# POETIC REFLECTIONS IN THE KEY OF LIFE

C D E F G A B C

Written by Dr. Bernard Mckenzie

ISBN: 978-1-969021-67-1 (ebook)
ISBN: 978-1-969021-65-7 (Paperback)
ISBN: 978-1-969021-66-4 (Hardcover)

# From the Author

These poems are a collection of the triumphs, defeats, and times of uncertainty we experience in this life. Granted, some of these poetic works are personal reflections and deal with my most intimate thoughts about life and our existence. Every day presents a new challenge or lesson to be learned, and thus, we must endure and persevere if we are to live our lives according to God's will. These poems look at the sovereignty of God. They look at the depth and assurance of His love.

His provision and protection and His control and guidance over circumstances that we are powerless without a solution. Prayerfully, upon reading these poetic works, you will be inspired and encouraged to trust completely in God and know that He loved us enough to sacrifice His only begotten Son, Jesus Christ, on our behalf and restore a relationship with Him we lost because of our sins. Life is not only how we take it but also what we make of it. God never forces us to obey, but sometimes, He will allow dire circumstances to humble us because of His love. Truthfully, He gives us a choice.

# Music Lesson

In music theory, a scale is an ascending and descending series of tones. I think that life is like a musical scale that starts from the first note called the tonic. And each note thereafter plays a part. The seventh note called the leading tone, should resolve to the last note, which is like the beginning note. This gives a feeling of completion. Music is written with many different keys, and each key has a unique sound. It may modulate or move through several different keys. But in a lot of compositions, it will go back to the beginning key it started in.

Each key presents a different tonality or feel, as each day presents a new challenge and response. In similarity, these poems are set to eight chapters. The first seven chapters capture certain experiences in our earthly existence. They look at the sovereignty of God and His faithfulness and love for man. They look at man's sin and our dependence on God as our creator, Father, and His love of sending his beloved son, Jesus Christ, who died for our sins. They look at our struggles and relationships with each other.

All the chapters look to salvation and deliverance, and we see Jesus as being man's deliverer and hope. The seventh chapter is climatic because it looks at some of my struggles or perhaps concerns about racial prejudices. It looks at some of the catastrophes we've had in recent years and how I was driven to write about what I saw. It pays tribute to certain individuals who have impacted my life and the lives of so many.

Chapter seven truly deals with some of my most intimate thoughts concerning life. Chapter seven resolves to the eighth chapter, which is like the beginning chapter when man had a loving relationship with God, our Creator. We were to live forever in paradise, never wanting for anything. But Satan deceived man, and because of our disobedience, we were tossed out of paradise. This last chapter speaks of a renewed relationship with God through our Lord Jesus Christ.

It is a guarantee that never again will we have to worry about the former things like sin, death, hatred, evil, and so many things we dealt with in our past. There will be a time of unspeakable joy in heaven, and we will have joy in worshiping before the throne of God.

# Table Of Contents

# Chapter One

"The Sovereignty of God and His love for man"

This chapter of the poems looks at the sovereignty of God and His love for man. God said that everything He created was good. He created man in His Image and gave him dominion over all living things. We were a special joy to God, but being tempted by Satan, we disobeyed God when we ate the forbidden fruit we were told to forsake. Because of our disobedience, we were kicked out of the Garden and sin entered the world, and death, sorrow, and trouble became our companions. But a loving God made a way for man to be restored through the precious blood of His only begotten Son, Jesus Christ. [ Genesis 3:15 and John 3: 16] Because of His love for us despite our weaknesses we should always be grateful and love Him because of His great mercy and compassion toward us. We should always praise Him for He is worthy of our praise. We can never repay Him because Jesus paid it all with His blood, and because of Him we shall have everlasting life and so shall we ever be with our Lord in Heaven, The New Jerusalem.

# "Thanks, Dear Lord, For This Day"

Thanks, dear Lord, for this day,
    Thank you for allowing me to greet the rising sun.

With the light in my eyes, I shall continually see,
    And give praise to the marvelous things you have done.

Last night I had a dream,
    That a bird of pure gold was singing just for you.

 And I was awakened by its melody.

The sweet vibrations gently cracked my window,
    Just enough for me to hear, and to know that you are near,

And just wanted to say, Thanks dear Lord, for this day.

**Rufus Mckenzie Jr.**

Taken from My deceased brother's book..." Poems of Faith"
Copyright 1991

"This is the day that the Lord has made; let us rejoice and be
glad in it." Psalm 118:24

# "Thank God for Today"

Yesterday's activity is all but gone,
What remains are thoughts of joy, sorrow, and pain.
The seeds of life in which we have sown,
Today's harvest is the fruit of that we have gain.

Farmers till the soil because they truly understand,
Stirring up the fresh dirt that lay beneath the ground.
The season of harvest will soon be upon their land,
Many will be fed, and hunger will not bound.

The mistakes made yesterday are seeded in our minds,
Today gives another chance, a time to correct or obey.
God's love and mercy is always available,
Shall we wait until tomorrow to thank Him? or shall we

Thank God For Today.

**Bernard Mckenzie**

Praise the Lord, give thanks to the Lord, for He is good; His
love endures forever. Psalms 106: 1 [NIV]

# "Praise God Anyway"

When things don't go the way we thought,
   Most times we run straight to God
Never conceding that it was probably your fault
   Now you complain about the trouble you bought

Your faith is tested and now to God you confide,
   Why Lord from me have you turn aside?
But yet in my distress, He heard my humble cry,
   For now I know a broken and contrite heart. He will not despise.

Regardless of your pain and trials that be,
   Be patient your deliverance is in your praise of thee.
For now, I know that no matter what problems I face day to day,
   I'm going to praise God anyway.

**Bernard Mckenzie**

"Give thanks in all circumstances, for this is the will of God in Christ Jesus for you" 1 Thessalonians 5:18 [ESV]

# "I Owe Thee"

For Adam's sin came down through men,
 Our hope was gone until love stepped in.
A love so broad I could not flee,
 For grace did save a wretch like me.

God's precious seed came upon her rest,
 A son she gave who was God's best.
The wiles of him that brought us low,
 Will always try to steal our souls.
Praise be to God for His sovereignty,
 The precious Son He gave for you and me,

Stained with sin but now redeemed,
 It was His blood that washed us clean.
Our treasures in Him will never rust,
 Thank God for His Son, Christ Jesus.
So now my lips will always be, the first to say
 I owe thee.

**Bernard Mckenzie**

"You were bought with a price [you were actually purchased with the precious blood of Jesus and made His own] So then, honor and glorify God with your body" 1 Corinthians 6.20 [AMP]

# "GOD LOVES YOU ANYWAY"

Why does God love sinners like us?
When all he asks is that only in him will we trust?
Always boasting on the things that we do right,
Never thanking God when we know it was his might.

Day in and day out, we walk as if alone.
He sees all our deeds and all our ways are known.
Man born of a woman, is of a few days and many troubles.
Surely God is ready to help us when our lives turn to rubble.

God is patient and to us his ways are sometimes strange
No one else is patient like him, to see our cold hearts change.
But God is love, and his mercy is new each and everyday

Despite of all your weaknesses," God loves you anyway.

**Bernard Mckenzie**

But God shows his love for us in that while we were still
sinners, Christ died for us. Romans 5. 8[ ESV]

6

# "It's Still God"

When I look at how the stars hang in the sky,
I know it was by his hand.
When I hear a baby's first cry,
I know it was He who created man.

When I see the dawning of another great day,
I know it is God who allows the sun to shine my way
When I escaped imminent danger and was unhurt
I know it was God who dispatched angels from heaven to
earth.

When I think about what all God has done,
I know his greatest gift is his precious son.
And without a doubt, I know it was and still is God.

**Bernard Mckenzie**

For his invisible attributes, namely, his eternal power and
divine nature, have been clearly perceived, ever since the
creation of the world, in the things that have been made. So,
they are without excuse. Romans 1: 20 [ESV]

7

# "I Am"

Oh, praise God, you who live,
Has any day passed when He doesn't give
The mornings you rise at dawns early light,
Remember it was God who kept you through the night.

Surely His throne is the world the creator of every living
thing.
But many have forsaken, His word and His reign.
The things we cherish now will soon fade away,
It will be as the dew that appears at the rising of each new
day.

We dare not trust things that will fade and rust,
And know without a doubt in God we can truly trust.
A loving God who sacrificed His Son as the perfect lamb,
For He that sent him is called "I Am."

**Bernard Mckenzie**

14 And God said unto Moses, I AM THAT I AM. and he said
Thus shalt thou say unto the children of Israel, I AM hath sent
me unto you. Exodus 3: 14 [KJV]

# "But God Does"

---

What if God doesn't love us?
What if God didn't feed us?
What if God doesn't lead us?
But God Does.

What if God doesn't know us?
What if God didn't show us?
What if God doesn't punish us?
But God Does.

What if God doesn't test us?
What if God doesn't bless us?
What if God doesn't mold us?
But God Does.

**Bernard McKenzie**

"We know how much God loves us because we have felt his love and because we believe him when he tells us that he loves us dearly. God is love, and anyone who lives in love is living with God and God is living in him. 1 John 16 (NLT)

# "That They May See"

So often we forget to thank our Lord for all He's done for us,
     Even the little things we take for granted, and all we do
is fuss.

A roof over our heads, food, and clothing we think is so small,
     But look at the those who have nothing at all.

A God who cares for all creation is worthy of all sur praise,
     In His hands is life, favor to all who follow His way.

Shall we love ourselves and continue to forsake our neighbors
     and disgrace our God above?
Or, shall we be His hands in service, so the world may see His
love.

**Bernard Mckenzie**

"Therefore, as God's chosen people, holy and dearly loved,
clothe yourselves with compassion, kindness, humility,
gentleness, and patience, Bear with each other and forgive one
another if any of you has a grievance against someone. Forgive
as the Lord forgave you. And over all these virtues put on love,
which binds them all together in perfect unity" Colossians
3:12-14 [NIV]

# "God Is Love"

Love creates.

Love dictates.

Love molds.

Love holds.

Love sees.

Love agrees.

Love cares.

Love bares.

Love corrects.

Love forgets.

Love bends.

Love amends.

Love raises.

Love praises.

Yet, in all of these things and more God is...

**Bernard McKenzie**

But God demonstrates his own love for us in this: While we were still sinners, Christ died for us. Romans 5:8 [NIV]

# "There Is Only One God"

What is this new scientific breakthrough in cloning life?
   Has man become so creative to put God's creatures under the knife? Certainly, God has endowed us with wisdom and understanding.
   But we say extinction and shortages have become more demanding.

Cows, birds, and all kinds of living things,
   Have succumb to what genetic science brings.
Have we forgotten who created the stars in the sky?
   Have we even considered the changes of seasons that passed by.

I don't believe our creator is pleased in what we've done?
   He said that I am a jealous God and beside me there is none.

**Bernard Mckenzie**

Unto thee it was shewed, that thou mightiest know that the LORD he is God; there is none else beside him... Deuteronomy 4: 35 [KJ]

# "Now I See"

Traveling blindly down life's highway.
I often heard people say.
How Jesus came and saved sinful man,
At first, I really couldn't understand.

And now every morning I rise,
How can I not see with my eyes.
That God so loved us to do such a thing,
In sacrificing His Son for us to be redeemed.

Surely, I won't forget the words I heard the people say,
Of the forgiveness we received that day,
When Jesus died for our sins on Calvary,
Yes, I was loss and blind, but now I see.

**Bernard Mckenzie**

Amazing grace, how sweet the sound That saved a wretch like me. I once was lost, but now I am found, Was blind, but now I see. (vs. 1 of Hymn. Amazin Grace

13

# Chapter Two

"Waiting On God'

So often in life's journey, we find ourselves stricken or struck by life's troubles. The Bible tells us in Job 14:1... A man born of a woman is of few days and full of trouble. It must be noted that some of our trouble comes because of our disobedience in adherence to God's word. In our call and cry for deliverance we seek God's mercy and deliverance. I believe it is these times we question God about our deliverance and urgency to move on our behalf in our time. We pray, but we get no immediate answer. We call and it seems that there is no connection. Surely, nothing is hidden from God, and He moves when He moves and nothing or no one can alter His will or decision. Thus, in waiting on God, we learn the meaning of being patient, humble, and repenting of our sins. Be encouraged because Isaiah 40:31 says that they that wait upon the Lord shall renew their strength, they shall mount up with wing as eagles, they shall run and not be weary, and walk and faint not. Are you the "they" in this scripture?

# "Not Long"

Lord how long? Will we sow from the harvest of our sins?
Lord how long before we'll be restored again?
Lord how long will we cry out in the night?
Lord how long will we be dismissed from your sight?

Lord how long must we wait to see your favor?
Lord how long will we do this hard, hard labor?
Lord how long before we go from test to bless?
Lord how long will we have to guess?

Lord, are we impatient and not willing to wait?
Lord, are we just too scared to ask in faith?
Lord we are not ready to suffer too long,
Lord, but all we hear you say is hold on, be strong, not long.


**Bernard Mckenzie**

How long, O LORD, must I call for help? But you do not listen
Violence is everywhere I cry, but you do not come to save.
Habakkuk 1:2-4 NLT]

# "WAIT ON GOD"

WAIT ON HIM, WHO REALLY DOES CARE,

WAIT ON HIM, YOUR BURDENS HE'LL BARE.

WAIT ON HIM, WHO CONTROLS ALL WE SEE,

WAIT ON HIM, WHO KNOWS ALL OUR NEEDS.

WAIT ON HIM, WHO CREATED THE LIGHT,

WAIT ON HIM, WHO RULES THE NIGHT,

WAIT ON HIM, WHO'S LOVE IS CALLED GRACE,

WAIT ON HIM, ONE DAY WE SHALL SEE HIS FACE,

JUST WAIT, BE PATIENT AND WAIT ON GOD.

**Bernard Mckenzie**

Wait for the Lord; Be strong and let your heart take courage.
Yes, wait for the Lord. Psalm 27.14 [NASB]

# "Your Trials Are Just A Test"

Gold shines now but at first it wasn't so,
From the earth It came, dressed as raw oar.
The refiner's fire came bursting through,
And now it shines anew.

The trials we face help make us strong,
And yet it we say it seems so long.
But hold your ground through fear and doubt,
God will surely bring you out.

Yes, life is joy and trouble as well,
Just don't give up or believe that you fail.
God will see your faithfulness in giving your best,
Your trials are just a test.

**Bernard Mckenzie**

These trials are only to test your faith, to see whether or not it is strong and pure. It is being tested as fire tests gold and purifies it and your faith is far more precious to God than mere gold, so, if your faith remains strong after being tried in the test tube of fiery trials, it will bring you much praise and glory and honor on the day of his return. 1 Peter 1:7-9 [LB]

# "THE MAKING OF YOU"

*TRIALS AND HARDSHIPS ARE TIMES THAT LIFE HOLD,*
*IT'S COMMON TO MAN, THE BRAVE AND THE BOLD.*
*OUR DAYS OF REBELLION, AND TIMES OF UNREST,*
*UNWISE CHOICES WHICH AT FIRST SEEMED BEST.*

*SEASONS CHANGE AS TIMES MOVES ON,*
*THE STORMY DAYS WE HOPE ARE GONE.*
*A SOVEREIGN LORD WHO CONTROLS ALL THINGS,*
*HE KNOWS THE TIMES AND WHAT EACH DAY BRINGS.*

*THE POTTERS WHEEL SHAPES ALL TYPES OF CLAY,*
*NO HEART IS SO STIFF THAT HE CANNOT SWAY.*
*HAVE FAITH IN GOD, AND YOU CAN BE MADE NEW,*
*THAT IS THE BEGINNING, IN THE MAKING OF YOU.*

**Bernard Mckenzie**

So, I went down to the potter's house, and there he was working at his wheel. And the vessel he was making of clay was spoiled in the potter's hand, and he reworked it into another vessel, as it seemed good to the potter to do. Jeremiah 18: 3-4 [ESV]

# "DON'T WORRY"

There will be trouble in life, and this we cannot sway,
> For earth has its pains from the beginning until
this day
These storms come in many ways and from them we cannot
flee.
> Our creator tells us to trust in him and says
don't worry.

Sometimes it's death, sorrow, and the tribulation of this world,
> But even so, God looks out for every man, woman, boy,
> and girl.
For it is He who calms the storms, and the waves that flurries,
> He still tells us to trust in him and says don't
worry.

He takes care of the birds, trees, and all living things we know,
> The world is his jewel, and man He loves so
When your storms come, please be patient and don't hurry,
> Your creator is telling you to trust in him and says
don't worry.

**Bernard McKenzie**

25 "Therefore I tell you, do not worry about your life, what
you will eat or drink, or about your body, what you will wear.
Is not life more than food, and the body more than clothes? 26
Look at the birds of the air, they do not sow or reap or store
away in barns, and yet your heavenly Father feeds them. Are
you not much more valuable than they? 27 Can any one of you
by worrying add a single hour to your life? Matthew 6: 25- 27
[NIV]

# "Why Worry?"

All of us find ourselves worrying about something on any given day, Forgetting that life is full of uncertainties, and often full of dismay.
The sun will rise without error or change, and is expected to be on, time, but when the trials of life come, we worry as if it is by design.

Jesus our savior knows all about the trouble that comes to harm us,
He is truly our burden bearer, and faith in him is trust.
He carries all our burdens, and no weight is too heavy for God's son,
Stop worrying and build your faith where there is none.

**Bernard Mckenzie**

Casting all your care upon him; for he careth for you. 1 Peter 57 [NIV]

# "Make Do"

How many times in life have you've said,
    I got to pay bills to keep a roof over my head.
When the pleasures in life seem so few,
    But what little you have you just "Make Do."

It's always nice to have much more than you need,
    A time of sharing and doing a good deed.
Sometimes we desire those things that are fresh and new,
    But having less will teach you how to "Make Do."

It's hard to be content with so little in hand,
    But what's more important for the survival of man.
God provides our needs as each day brings dew,
    There will be times of plenty, but for now you just "Make
Do."

**Bernard McKenzie**

11 Not that I was ever in need, for I have learned how to be content with whatever I have.
Philippians 4:11

# "Deliverance At Dawn"

Of each glaring moment of what life gives,
There is a defining moment to all who live.
A time of sorrow, joy, and times of waiting.
Always knowing that our time is fading.

Nature's change is set by the creator of all,
Even the dew drops are measured that fall.
Nothing that happens is not known by Him,
He knows each star before it goes dim.

Our victories are the fruits of the trials we shall see,
No glory is upon those who give in to defeat,
As each new day begins with a sigh of our yawn,
The God who love's us is our guiding light at dawn.

**Bernard Mckenzie**

When morning dawned, the angels urged Lot, saying, "Up, take your wife and your two daughters who are here, or you will be swept away in the punishment of the city, Genesis 19:15 [NIV]

# "A Second Chance"

I have a second chance in life to do what I've always wanted
to do,
> There are many people that feel the same as I.
> > Then yet there are few.

A second chance to spread the gift of love to show that I really
do care, A second chance to realize that my God will
always be there.

**Rufus Mckenzie Jr.**

Taken from My deceased brother's book..." Poems of Faith"
Copyright 1991
"I love the Lord because he hears me, He listens to my prayers.
He listens to me every time I call to Him." Psalm 116: 1-2

# "Faith"

God's promises are sure in every way,
  From the beginning of time, at the dawn of each new day.
If the things we desire are in His will,
  We must patiently wait because God says to be still.

God's word will endure through all of eternity,
And those who trust in Him shall find prosperity.
Why do we value things we need to survive?
It will never compare what's not seen by our eyes.

Yes, patience is required while waiting on God,
His ways are not determined by what we think is hard.
God's word is life for all who believe,
For they shall be blessed, and they shall receive.

**Bernard Mckenzie**

Now faith is the substance of things hoped for, and the evidence of things not seen. Hebrews 11:1 [KJ] And without faith it is impossible to please God because anyone who comes to him must believe that he exists and that he rewards those who earnestly seek him. Hebrews 11: 6[NIV]

# "It's Only Temporary."

The trials will come to test your faith.,
In them we learn how to wait.
The hope that keeps us singings songs of Joy.
Will help keep us when trouble comes to destroy.

Waves that splash up against the sandy shores,
Return over and over to gather more.
Words and deeds will one day cease,
But God's love for you will never decrease

These earthly vessels do ache with life's pain,
But our dependence on God is ours to gain.
Though life's storms dim the brightest of days,
It's only temporary, for your deliverance is on the way.

**Bernard Mckenzie**

"Consider it pure joy, my brothers, and sisters, whenever you face trials of many kinds, because you know that the testing of your faith produces perseverance. Let perseverance finish its work so that you may be mature and complete, not lacking anything." James 1: 2-4 [NIV]

# "This Too Shall Pass"

The wilderness in life comes to all that live,
    Times of grief, sorrow, and weariness it gives.
Have faith in the hand that calms the waters.
    Christ Jesus came to put at things in order.

We must dare not wallow in life's pain and hurt,
    For there will be a new heaven and earth.
For in Jesus we move and have our being.
    Peace and eternal life will be our healing.

This Poem I write brings joy to my heart,
    Even through hard trials, I shall not depart.
Surely, whatever trials we face won' last,
    Just hold on because this to shall pass.

**Bernard Mckenzie**

For this light momentary affliction is preparing for us an eternal weight of glory beyond all comparison, as we look not to the things that are seen but to the things that are unseen. For the things that are seen are transient, but the things that are unseen are eternal 2 Corinthians 4 17-18 [ESV]

# Chapter Three

"Encouragement is Healing"

Many times, in this life all of us are faced with new trials, and sometimes encouragement is exhibited in those who have overcome similar circumstances that are new and devastating to you now. A testimony from those who are delivered bears credibility to the awesome power and salvation of our Lord and Savior, Jesus Christ. In the life of the believer, we must walk in this Christian experience together. Hebrews 10:25 tells us not to give up meeting together, as some are in the habit of doing, but let us encourage one another. Together we find strength, love, hope, and a renewal of our purpose to do and obey God's will. A word of encouragement, a hug, or a listening ear is a form of spiritual healing to the sad, the hurt, and the discouraged. Sometimes in life, we come to crossroads as well as back roads, and a word from God and a hug are all that's needed. Let us continue to look at each day as an opportunity to tell somebody that you love them and about God's love for them as well.

# "Don't Give Up"

I know your pain, when you're down,
Maybe it's your trouble, that has you bound.
When life seems hard and you've had enough,
But please! Whatever you do, don't give up.

Your testimony might be the one that breaks,
The chains on someone who find it hard to shake,
Deliverance is coming, even though it's tough.
But please! Whatever you do, don't give up.

The joy, sorrow, peace, and pain,
In life It shall come like the sun and rain.
Just trust and wait on God, who fills our cup,
But please! Whatever you do, don't give up.

**Bernard McKenzie**

Rejoice in hope, be patient in tribulation, be constant in prayer
Romans 12.12 [ESV]

# "REJOICE, YOUR SPRING IS COMING"

THE LEAVES FALL AND SHED THEIR GREENS,
THE GRASS WITHERS FOR A TIME IT SEEMS.
SEASONS CHANGE FOR ALL LIVING THINGS,
YET NEW LIFE WILL COME IN THE SEASON WE
CALL SPRING.

FOR A TIME, WE'LL SEE MUCH JOY IN OUR DAYS,
AS WELL AS THE PAIN AND SORROW THAT LAY.
TRUST IN GOD WHO SUPPLIES ALL OF YOUR NEEDS,
HE KNOWS OUR WAYS, AND AWARE OF OUR DEEDS.

LIFE WILL BE ETERNAL FOR ALL WHO BELIEVE,
IN CHRIST AND HIS DEATH ON A HILL CALL
CALVARY.
SPRING WILL NOT COME TO THOSE WHO DENY
GOD'S SON,
HE IS RISEN SO REJOICE, YOUR SPRING IS COMING.

**Bernard Mckenzie**

Be patient, then, brothers and sisters, until the Lord's coming.
See how the farmer waits for the land to yield its valuable crop,
patiently waiting for the autumn and spring rains. James 5:7
[NIV]

29

# "Time Will"

TIME WILL HEAL A BROKEN HEART,

TIME WILL SAY IT'S TIME TO DEPART.

TIME WILL TELL THE SEASONS TO BEGIN AND END,

TIME WILL MAKE THE OCEAN GO OUT AND COME IN.

TIME WILL HELP OUR FAITH TO GROW,

TIME WILL TELL OUR SORROWS NO MORE.

TIME WILL NEVER STAY THE SAME,

TIME WILL DICTATE OUR GOALS AND OUR AIMS.

TIME WILL SEE OUR LIGHTS GO DIM,

TIME WILL HELP STRENGTHEN OUR FAITH IN HIM.

TIME WILL SEE OUR VALLEYS AND OUR HILLS,

AND WHATEVER HAPPENS TIME WILL.

**Bernard Mckenzie**

1 There is a time for everything, and a season for every activity under the heavens: Ecclesiastes 3: 1 [NIV]

# "When Morning Comes`!"

Awake and rejoice to the dawning of a new day,
Even through your midnight, God watched while you lay.
He created the sun to shine on His creation,
And sacrificed His Son for the sins of all nations.

Nothing will ever separate His Love toward us,
Jesus is our savior, and in Him only shall we trust.
Many have gone asleep, but morning will come as well,
Life for all will be eternal, either heaven or hell.

While we still have breath, lets us praise God from whom all blessings flow,
and thank Him for sending Jesus, For He is the door.
A heavenly home awaits the faithful, or a place called hell for some.
Your choice will determine your destination, so where will you be?
When morning comes.

**Bernard Mckenzie**

Because of the tender mercy of our God,

With which the Sunrise from on high will visit us,

To shine upon those who sit in darkness and the shadow of death,

To guide our feet into the way of peace." Luke 1: 78-79

# "Happy Again"

Even happy times will sometimes turn sad,
  Replacing the joy and laughter you once had.
The walls that now seem so hard to climb,
  Will be a testimony forever carved in your mind.

Promises that are made will sometimes be broken.
  Trusting in someone, and the chances that are taken.
No one day is the same and this we know,
  The heart is a mirror that reflects our inner glow.

The hurt and pain that never seems to go away,
  Shall be like the mist and the dawn of each new day.
Don't worry about circumstances you can't foresee.
  Your sun is rising and soon you will be...

**Bernard Mckenzie**

And after you have suffered a little while, the God of all grace,
who has called you to his eternal glory in Christ, will himself
restore, confirm, strengthen, and establish you. 1 Peter 5:10
[NIV]

# "RETURN TO ME"

You left home when things look so bright,
With your treasures, good health, and a smile of light.
But oh, darkness came, and your joy became dim,
And now you ponder, broke and disgusted, should I return to
him?

Now you know that it was God who kept you,
But trouble came to undo what no man could do.
And now with your head down and no where to hide,
Just look upward for your help, in God you can confide.

He stretched out his hand and called you by name,
To let you know that in Him there is no shame
A loving father who shows compassion and mercy,
Tells you to come home and "return to me."

**Bernard McKenzie**

22 But the father said to his servants, Bring quickly the best robe, and put it on him, and put a ring on his hand, and shoes on his feet. And bring the fattened calf and kill it, and let us eat and celebrate. 24 For this my son was dead, and is alive again, he was lost, and is found. And they began to celebrate. Luke 15:22-24 [NIV]

# "God's Unchanging Love"

The loss of a loved one is news we dread and fear,
But life teaches us that death takes from us those so dear.
A day of joy is often followed by a moment of sorrow,
Praying that the pain we feel will dissipate by tomorrow.

The sorrow you feel is truly known by God, who forever
sustains us,
But thanks be to God that death has no sting because of our
lord and savior Jesus.
Jesus died to save us and give us power to succeed,
In him life is everlasting and comfort to those who are
bereaved.

Even though this is a time of unforgettable grief,
God is always with us when death comes as a thief.
May your joy be uplifted as you gain strength from above,
Nor
death or anything else can separate us from God's
unchanging love.

**Bernard McKenzie**

38 For I am persuaded, that neither death, nor life, nor angels,
nor principalities, nor powers, nor things present, nor things to
come,
39 Nor height, nor depth, nor any other creature, shall be able
to separate us from the love of God, which is in Christ Jesus
our Lord. Romans 8: 38-39 (KJV)

# "Faith Is The Key"

Words cannot ease the grief you feel,
Some say it's useless, yet some they will.
But know that this life, is not the end of man's story,
There will be a new life in hell's abyss, or in heavens glory.

The memories we have of those that have passed on,
Is etched in our hearts, our lips, and our songs,
Though we are left behind with the scars of our grief,
We must not tarry for death will come as a thief.

Make your decision and receive Jesus Christ today,
He is the only one that can stand in death's way.
Now as you ponder in what to truly believe,
Maybe it would help to know that Jesus is the answer, and
your faith is the key.

**8.** But what does it say? "The word is near you, it is in your
mouth and in your heart," that is, the word of faith we are
proclaiming; 9. That if you confess with your mouth, Jesus is
Lord, and believe in your heart that God raised Him from the
dead, you will be save. Romans 10.8- 9[BSB]

**Bernard McKenzie**

# "The Joy of The Lord Is Our Strength."

Every day presents unseen obstacles and circumstances we must bear, we can cast our all our burdens on the one and only God that cares.
The times of rest after the toil of our daily labor,
is a refreshing moment that is to be enjoyed and savored.

Our homes, jobs, and everything that we cherish as such,
will all at times seem heavy and sometimes too much.
But O' thank God that even when the days are well spent,
let your heart sing out with gladness because the joy of the Lord is our strength.

**Bernard Mckenzie**

"The Lord is my strength and my shield, my heart trusts in him, and he helps me. My heart leaps for joy, and with my song I praise him. "Psalm 28:7[NIV]

# "The Awakening"

To Be Sleep Means More That Resting One's Eyes,
It's Pride And Stubbornness Something God Despise.
Man Thinks He Has The Power That Makes Everything Go,
Only Realizing His Mortal Weaknesses When Trouble Is At
The Door.

Tell Me What It Will Take For Us To Truly Know?
That All Creation Is In God's Hands, And He Loves Us So.
Death And Disasters And All That Come To Pass.
Reminds Us That Only In God's Love Can We Last.

Will It Take Losing Something or Someone for Us to See,
That Jesus Gives Eternal Life and Life Abundantly.
Do We Ignore God's Son and The Signs of These Last Days,
Or, Will This Be the Day of Your Awakening.

**Bernard Mckenzie**

*"Lift Up Your Eyes And Look To The Heavens. Who Created*
*All These? He Who Brings Out The Starry Host One By One*
*And Calls Forth Each Of Them By Name. Because Of His*
*Great Power And Mighty Strength, Not One Of Them Is*
*Missing "Isaiah 40: 26 (NIV)*

37

# "Life And Death"

The joy of witnessing the birth of a newborn child,
Is truly a miracle that we can only cherish a little while.
A flower that grows and is adorned with such radiant beauty,
Soon withers and falls to earth after its intendent duty.

All living things will have a day of glory and worth,
They will leave a seed that continues to sprout new birth.
From humans and even the tiniest of all living things,
Will come to know that life will be as fall is to spring.

Even knowing that life will end for all in some way,
Is never easy when it comes to that day.
God gave life to man by the blowing of His breath,
And it is God who holds the key to life and death.

**Bernard Mckenzie**

For since death came through a man, the resurrection of the dead comes also through a man. 1 Corinthians 15:21

# "Your Loss Is God's Gain"

It's hard when death takes those we love,
And the only comfort is from our father above.
Though we offer words of love with deep sympathy,
It may not be enough for the heart that is so heavy.

The days of our earthly journey are all so few,
God has numbered our days like every drop of dew.
Our time must be spent wisely with each fleeting day,
We don't know what tomorrow may bring our way.

Even death as we know it is not completely done,
Everlasting life can only be obtained in Jesus, God's son.
And when it seems that nothing else will ease your pain,
Maybe it's comforting to know that your loss is God's gain.

**Bernard Mckenzie**

psalms 116:15
"precious in the sight of the Lord is the death of his saints"

# "We Have The Victory"

Hearing of the loss of a love one is news we rather not hear,
It reminds us of how each moment of life is so precious, and
so dear.
The tears that fall are caught by God, who knows our earthly
sorrow,
In Him is true comfort and strength, and hope for the day
called tomorrow.

The loved ones we cherish in our minds and hearts are very
difficult to lose,
But God gave up his only begotten son, and now there is
"Good News"
Though the grave may hold us temporarily, it will never boast
too long,
The salvation that's only found in Jesus secures our eternal
home.

The thoughts, cards and words may help to ease your pain,
Death is no respecter of person, and it knows our names.
If there are any words of comfort, that's offered during this sad
time,
May you find joy in knowing that in Jesus, "The Victory Shall
Be Mine?"

**Bernard Mckenzie**

He will wipe away every tear from their eyes, and death shall
be no more, neither shall there be mourning, nor crying, nor
pain anymore, for the former things have passed away.
"Revelation 21.4

40

# "We Are Our Brother's Keeper."

The hugs, letters and deeds that may seem so small,
Is more precious than gold to those who've lost it all.
The sorrow and sadness that life brings is real,
These times create opportunities to show love and good will.

Though our days are often full of joy and laughter,
Is sometimes followed with trouble and disaster.
A Day of sunshine that dries up yesterdays pain,
Will be a day of comfort that the hurting has gain.

The tragedy of the story of Cain and Abel,
Reminds us we must love and not envy our neighbor.
Maybe your kindness can help one from falling deeper,
Because in God's eye we are our brother's keeper.

But whoever has the world's goods, and sees his brother in
need and closes his heart against him, how does the love of
God abide in him? Little children, let us not love with word or
with tongue, but in deeds and truth. 1 John3 17-18[NIV]

**Bernard Mckenzie**

# "A Poem For Comfort And Grief"

In your grief, keep your belief, that God comforts those who mourn,
Even though we all know that at times like these, it's very hard to stay strong.

But remember too that He also realizes that another precious life is gone.

**Rufus Mckenzie Jr.**

Taken from My deceased brother's book..." Poems of Faith" Copyright 1991

"Precious in the sight of the Lord is the death of His faithful ones. Psalm 116: 15 [NRSV]

# "Home Sweet Home"

Some things in life remain a mystery,
Trials and loss of loved ones are now recorded in history.
Though we grieve and ask the question why?
God knows our sorrow and catches the tears from our eyes.

The comforting words and prayers after losing one so dear,
Helps in times when no one else is near.
Yes, our earthly suffering is heaven's gain,
The God that gave life, takes it all the same.

Never will you forget the times you had together,
The laughter, and joy you shared when times were better.
Though we feel like we are left alone,
Rest assured in God's arms "Little Pam" is saying.
Don't cry y'all, I'm home sweet home.

**Bernard Mckenzie**

Written For Bob and Pam in memory of their deceased daughter "Lil" Pam.

# "Hospice Is Not The End."

Being made comfortable, and told that your journey is almost done,
Is something the receiver of this news knows is not fun.
We must know our time on earth is numbered and inevitable,
And to the terminally ill, the thought of dying is almost unbearable.

Life is something we want to hold on to until our last breath,
Because of our fall from grace in the Garden of Eden, we shall all face death.
But a loving and merciful God made a way for us to escape eternal condemnation,
Because of Jesus 'death on Calvary, all who put their faith in him shall receive salvation.

Though the curtains are about to close on this part of your earthly journey,
There is comfort in knowing that in Christ is life for all eternity.
Even the fear of knowing that the life you live or lived is stained with sin,
Maybe now is the right time to receive Jesus because Hospice is not the end.

**Bernard Mckenzie**

# Chapter Four

## "GO YE THEREFORE, OH CHRISTIAN"

Before Jesus ascended back to Heaven, He commissioned us to take the message of salvation to the ends of the earth. He assured us that regardless of suffering or opposition, He will always be with us until the end. Matthew 28: 19-20. In a world full of sin, hate, rebellion, and evil that surrounds us daily, Christians are torchbearers of the gospel, the good news about Christ. It is Satan's mission to destroy or sabotage God's will for man, and we must be strong in the Lord and the power of his might. Ephesians 6:10, "For our battle is not against flesh and blood, but against principalities, against powers, against the rulers of the darkness of this age, against spiritual hosts of wickedness in the heavenly places." Remember Jesus is always with you. Be ye steadfast, immovable, always abounding in the work of the Lord, 1 Corinthians 15:58.

# "The Battlefield"

Where is your faith, you who doubt?
    When trials came, God brought you out.
Even though you claimed that you were healed,
    You must not forget, that evil is real.

As soldiers, we tread this world of wrongs,
    Bringing the lost to our savior's arms.
In Jesus we move and have our being,
    The paradise He promised will be worth seeing.

Through dangers seen and evil all around,
    We press onward towards the joy we've found
Shine up your armor, your sword and shield,
    You oh Chistian are on the battlefield.

**Bernard Mckenzie**

Song refrain: Onward Christian Soldiers
Refrain:
Onward, Christian soldiers,
marching as to war
With the cross of Jesus
going on before

But watch thou in all things, endure afflictions, do the work of
an evangelist, make full proof of thy ministry. 2 Timothy 4.5
[NIV]

# "Hail To A Soldier"

The memories I have of her will always be,
Of how she stayed on the battlefield for thee.
Teaching, Loving and always steadfast,
To the work of God whose love will forever last.

Those she trained have much to say,
In their youth of how she went out her way.
In discipline and love, she was never slack,
She always brought something sweet in her sack.

When trials came, she was stern as tree,
Her love for the church was real as could be.
She trusted God with all her heart,
She knew His love toward her would never depart.

The saving of souls was her battle cry,
In Jesus she knew that we'll never die.
She was truly a mother to all who knew her,
For truly this poem is a tribute, and hail to a soldier"

**Bernard Mckenzie**

This poem is a tribute to our deceased Mother Jessie Copeland,
the beloved mother of Sanctuary Historically Cannan Hill
Missionary Baptist Church in Montgomery Alabama

# "Torchbearers"

Praise God for you who go out in his name,
Sharing the gospel without fear or shame.
The trials, troubles and turmoils you face,
Is small compared to God's mercy and grace.

The joy in seeing the lost being found,
From the shores of darkness that had them bound
For they too must carry the torch of God's desire,
That no one should be cast into the eternal fire.

The race is on and we shall win,
Jesus promised to be with us until the end
The day is now and we need not tarry,
The gospel message is what we'll carry

The saints of the past, who set the course,
Found strength in Jesus and had no remorse.
They believed God's word is true without errors,
We too must continue to be God's "Torchbearers.

**Bernard McKenzie**

**Dedicated to**

**Pastor Paul and Carolyn Wilde**
**And New Life In Christ Church**

**In celebration of the book, <u>Torchbearers</u>, written by**
**Carolyn**
**Wilde.**

# "Lest We Forget, How We Got Over"

The Children of Israel, who crossed the Red Sea,
From Egypt through the wilderness, God cared for thee,
On the shore of the Jordan, they camped by night,
Looking to Jericho in the hand of thy might.

They brought the ark and laid the twelve stones,
Their children shall remember, they were not alone.
No sea, no wall or army of great number,
Can battle with our God, who never sleeps or slumber.

The God of yesterday is the same God today,
His love is eternal for those who obey.
The rivers of life will come as we stand,
But the children of God will cross on dry land.

Our deliverer has come, in him we abide,
Redeeming our souls, for us Jesus died.
For now, we lean with our head on his shoulder,
"Lest We Forget, How We Got Over"

**Bernard McKenzie**

Jesus Christ is the same yesterday and today and forever.
Hebrews 13. 8 [NIV]

# "The Great Commission"

How can we rest when souls are still lost?
Thinking only of ourselves, and what it may cost.
Shouting glory! Glory! I'm glad I'm saved!
While sinners do plunge, deep in their graves

This gospel we preach sounds good to our ear,
But what good is it, if the unsaved cannot hear.
We must tell the world that God has forgiven,
Through Jesus the Christ, now life is worth living.

Surely, no four walls, can hold this true story,
How Jesus died and rules now in glory.
So be not dismayed, if they dare not listen,
You've sowed your seed in "The Great Commission."

**Bernard Mckenzie**

19 Therefore go and make disciples of all nations, baptizing them in the name of the Father and of the Son and of the Holy Spirit, 20 and teaching them to obey everything I have commanded you. And surely, I am with you always, to the very end of the age. "Matthew 28: 19-20

# "Preach The Word"

You who preach the word in season and out,
   To ears that are hardened and those who doubt.
Don't be discouraged if God's word is not heard,
   But you must continue to preach the word.

In sin and rebellion of those who may laugh,
   Will receive the benefit of God's wrath.
True repentance is a change for the best.
   Especially in Christ if they confess.

Miracles, signs and wonders they do see,
Some say it's magic and they'll never believe.
Don't be discouraged if God's word is not heard,
Oh man of God, you must continue to preach the word.

**Bernard Mckenzie**

Preach the word of God. Be prepared, whether the time is favorable or not. Patiently correct, rebuke, and encourage your people with good teaching. 2 Timothy 2: 4 [NLT]

# "The Fields"

Think of farmers who seed the ground and look to times of
harvest,
But we who know the gospel news find ourselves at rest.
God has made a way for man that all can be redeemed
Though Jesus Christ His only Son, His blood has washed us
cleaned.

We who have put our faith in Christ, must spread the word
around, Telling the world of our savior's love, and the eternal
life we've found The fields are ripe and ready to glean, and
we must be God's voice,
To tell the world that Jesus Christ has pal it all, and now we
can rejoice.

**Bernard Mckenzie**

35 And Jesus went throughout all the cities and villages,
teaching in their synagogues and proclaiming the gospel of the
kingdom and healing every disease and every affliction. 36
When he saw the crowds, he had compassion for them,
because they were harassed and helpless, like sheep without a
shepherd. 37 Then he said to his disciples, "The harvest is
plentiful, but the laborers are few, 38 therefore pray earnestly
to the Lord of the harvest to send out laborers into his harvest."
Matthew 9: 35-38 | ESV]

# "I'm Tired"

Ye Servant of the Lord where have you been?
I looked for you last Sunday to hug you again.
I called you at home to see what happen to you,
But all I keep hearing is that you are through.

Where is the joy that once glowed on your face?
The song we sung called amazing grace.
You were so proud to do what you admired,
But now all I hear you say is I'm tired.

**Bernard Mckenzie**

This poem is written in honor of those who served in the Church. As a minister and child of God I understand some of the difficulties in working in ministry. Those who lose or have lost their joy in serving are sometimes overworked and underappreciated. In Matthew 9: 37- 38. Jesus said... 37 Then he said to his disciples, "The harvest is plentiful, but the laborers are few, 38 therefore pray earnestly to the Lord of the harvest to send out laborers into his harvest." That is why in the body of Christ that the work of the ministry be shared by all and not just a few members who hold several positions in the Church. The Church is one body, but many members. Each member is endowed with a specific spiritual gift to edify the body of Christ. This allows the ministry to function effectively. No member should be a part or over everything. For those who find themselves in this predicament, be encouraged and know that your labor is not in Vain... (1 Corinthians 15.58]

# Chapter Five

"Personal reflections"

This series of poems is based on personal, and various life occurrences and experiences that will always be etched in our minds, as well as our hearts. In Music, the fifth note of a scale is called dominant because it is the second in importance to the first or last notes of a scale. This chapter highlights certain life-changing circumstances. The loss of loved ones, the tragic events that have a profound impact on the individual, a nation, or society as a whole, also in this series, I've written poems in honor of special people in my life, and to encourage the families of the dearly departed. The human existence is full of emotions, triumphs as well as defeats.

Ecclesiastes 3:1, it states "To everything, there is a season, and a purpose, and a time for every purpose under heaven." These poems recognize the values which are important to our spiritual and physical development. To be loved, or praised for a job well done. To be sympathetic in time of need We are never to forget that all of us have an important role in the lives of each other. These poems honor those who gave their lives to preserve or enhance a better quality of life for others. As we reflect on life-altering experiences, let us always remember that God is love, and we should be willing vessels ready to reflect this same love to the world in our service.

# "My Family"

I thank God for a wonderful family,
The sharing and caring that's displayed unselfishly.
Surely there are days when things are not the brightest,
But love keeps us together when things are the tightest.

Our days together are precious jewels of life,
What God has blessed, will never be destroyed by strife.
The anger that comes, only last temporarily,
Forgiveness is forgetting, and prayer is necessary.

My wife, children, and even the pets in my home,
Trust in the Lord who guides us through dangers unknown.
Regardless of trials and troubles that will be,
I thank God for such a wonderful family.

**Bernard Mckenzie**

**This poem is dedicated to the institution of the family and
the importance of the love that is shared unconditionally.**

# "A Tribute To My Mother"

The memories of those childhood days,
  Only she loved and knew my ways.
The voice of hers I remember so clear,
Momma was always watching me and always near.

Never forgetting how she always carried me,
In Joy, sadness and whatever it might be.
She showed God's love as best as she could,
Even when she chastised me, she said it was good.

She loved to sing about her Lord so much,
Always encouraging others and those she touched.
Her gifted voice touch many a soul,
Now heaven is blessed and waiting to behold

Yes, the curtains have closed and now she rests,
In a place called paradise enjoying God's best.
The love my mother gave was like no other,
This truly is a tribute to my mother

**Bernard Mckenzie**

This poem was written in memory of Mrs. Willie M. Baxter
who died October 19, 2003. It was given to Mrs. Grace Brown
and family.

# "A Wonderful Wife"

Several years have come and gone,
With you by my side, I'm never alone.
Through joy, sorrow, and all that we share,
If no one else cares, I know you'll be there.

Encouraging words that whisper in my ear,
Only God and you know, the depth of my fears.
Thanks be to God, for I am truly blessed,
To have someone like you, in this I profess.

The caring, sharing, and all that you do,
You cover our family and home like the morning dew.
If I never say anything else worthwhile in my life,
I just need you to know that you are truly a wonderful wife.

**Bernard Mckenzie**

This poem is a tribute to my beautiful wife Mrs. Addie Rippy
who really is my better half and I thank God for her. It is also
a tribute to all wives who deserved recognition for what they
are to their spouse and family.

# "Grandparents"

When I think about grandparents, I know that God lives,
   From their love, compassion, and willingness to forgive.

Nothing I do or say could ever change their love for me,
   I could do just about anything, and they say let me be.

They remind me so much of how God loves us so much,
   Even in our sins, He sent his son Jesus to die for us.

Yes, I will always treasure my memory of their love,
   For I know they are with Jesus, in heaven above.

**Bernard Mckenzie**

We all probably can remember growing up as children and being able to spend time with our Grandparents. I remember how loving and compassionate my grandparents were. I could get away with things that normally my mother or father would punish me for. But my grandparents were like "Leave that baby alone he'll be okay" I was like thank you Granny, or Grandpa. They had a forgiving love no matter how bad you were, and this is the Love God has for us in sending Jesus to die for our sins... We can always find compassion and forgiveness in Him.

For God so loved the world that he gave His only begotten Son to die for our sins and whoever shall believe in Him shall not perish but have everlasting life
John 3: 16

# 'MY Father And My Friend"

As I look back over time, during those growing-up years,
Dad always provided for us and calmed all our fears.
Though sometimes he was stern and always fair,
Later I realized it was because he cared.

Never did we hunger, nor anything did we lack,
His example was that we would learn to give back.
He loved the Lord, and that was his humble cry,
We will never forget him, though we say goodbye.

He has finished this race, and goes to receive his crown,
Singing Glory Halleluiah, oh what joy I've found.
Surely, I'll see him when our savior comes again,
But for now, I'll always remember, "My Father and My
Friend."

**Bernard McKenzie**

**DEDICATED TO:**
**PASTOR TERRY ELLISON AND FAMILY**
**IN MEMORY OF**

**FATHER DEACON EARNEST ELLISON**

# "The Apple of My Eye"

How could I forget this beautiful lady of love,
She knows more about me except for God above.
For many days and years, she toiled to keep us afloat,
And now I salute her, for she's worthy to note.

All those days she worked so hard to provide,
But ultimately, I know it was God on her side.
She could cook a little food, and that was plenty,
It reminded me of the miracle when Jesus fed many.

I remember getting up with her as she went to work,
Five o'clock in the morning, even in misery and hurt.
Those early days in school were very hard sometimes,
Neighborhood bullies who would take Mama's hard-earned
dime.

She always stressed the importance of an education,
The degree on my wall is from her dedication.
Through hard times or struggles, she never questioned God
why,
My mother will always be "The Apple of My Eye."

**Bernard Mckenzie**

In tribute to my wonderful mother, Mrs. Alberta Benekin
Mckenzie whom I love very much. She deserves more credit
and praise than I could ever write about. This poem is also in
respect, a tribute to all mothers.

"Honor your father and mother" (this is the first
commandment with a promise), Ephesians 6: 2 (ESV]

# "MY DAD"

Those precious memories that seemed just yesterday,
Birth the joy only he could bring my way.
Never will I forget the love, joy, and protection in him,
with my dad, my days were never dim.

Those strong arms were so gentle when he touched,
Gave me a sense of security that meant so much.
Though he goes to be with the creator of all mankind,
I will truly miss him because he was mine.

It is said that a daughter is the greatest gift to a man,
The things he did for me only I could understand.
Surely, I will miss him and sometimes be sad,
But the precious memories that bring joy will always be of my
dad.

**Bernard McKenzie**

Written for Mrs. Thelma Woolfolk, a friend and co-worker at
Alabama State University during the loss of her Father

# "Rufus The Harmonica Man"

As children, we had no idea of what or who we wanted to be,
We were always told a pot of Gold was under the rainbow tree.
My dad would play his harmonica and sing songs of old news,
We would laugh and say maybe this is the music they called
the
blues.

I never thought that I would play music and sing like my dad,
But as time passed, I said this music thing I inherited was not
that
bad.
Yes, my laughter reminds me of the joy we had during those
years, Thinking of my gifted father and how his music calmed
our fears.

Yes, I know in heaven they called him Rufus the harmonica
man,
He always played and sang by himself as a one-man band.
Dad thank you for giving me the gift to continue your story,
Now you sing and play with the angels giving God the glory.

**Bernard Mckenzie**

This poem is a tribute to my deceased father Rufus Mckenzie.
He was truly a musical pioneer who many years ago I and my
siblings thought he was funny and perhaps a little crazy. We
would go places and he would whip out that Harmonica and
we felt so embarrassed. Like Dad please don't do this. It was
later that we all realized that the music he was playing was
historic early blues. It can now be purchased on Apple iTunes.
Thank you, Dad, for your love and the many years you kept us
laughing.

# "Our Love"

As we walk down this path in the power of love,
We are blessed and know it's ordained from above.
As the sunshine comes to dry the dew of each new day,
Let our love be the strength that guides our way

For we know the rain will come, and darkness will fill the sky,
But our love will overcome the storms, and they will soon pass by.
May the light in our hearts burn and never go out,
Let our love be everlasting and never be in doubt.

The years will pass by, and nothing will remain the same,
Lord, let our love forever be strong, and it will never change.
For whatever reason in life that we may be apart,
Lord, let your love keep us and be the strength in our hearts.

**Bernard Mckenzie**

This poem was a gift for Rev. Dr. Rory L. Kent Sr. and Mary Kent. Rev. Kent is now the Pastor of The First Missionary Baptist Church in Greenville, Alabama. I had the privilege of officiating their wedding ceremony on September 27, 2020. They are truly close friends I admire.

# "The Two Shall Become as One"

From the very beginning, it was God's will,
The bonding of a man and woman to fulfill.
To have dominion over the things of this earth,
Becoming the union that will give new birth.

How blessed are they to have a family and home,
For God said it was not good for man to be alone.
Yes, some days are trying for both,
But we must always remember the precepts of our oath.

For better or worse, until death do us part,
Will only be kept in the depths of our hearts.
The pain, sorrow and many trials under the sun,
Will have no victory when the two shall become as one.

**Bernard Mckenzie**

23 And Adam said, this is now bone of my bones and flesh of my flesh: she shall be called Woman because she was taken out of Man.

24 Therefore shall a man leave his father and his mother and shall cleave unto his wife: and they shall be one flesh. Genesis 2: 23-24 (KJV)

# "Our Dearest "Bert"

Though the sting of death has taken her away,
it'll never overshadow my joy in remembering my friend
today.
Reflecting many years ago while in school at ASU,
Bert would always tell me ways of how to make it through.

She had many talents that the Lord surely gave, but when you
stepped on Bert's toe, she would tell you." now you better
behave."
She was also a great organizer, gifted writer, an excellent cook,
and so
much more,
But now she rests from her earthly labor, and we will miss her
so.

To Family, friends and all the bereaved, may you be
comforted in knowing that Bert has been received,
To a place where trouble will no longer exist, and the weary
shall find relief,

Though our sorrow may well up in tears, and fall to the earth,
    May our joy be rekindled, when we remember "our
dearest BERT"

**Rev. Bernard Mckenzie**

* This poem was presented to the late Mrs. Victoria Haigler
and family members. Written in memory of Mrs. Alberta
Davis who departed us on October 6, 2005. Bert as we know
her was a gift to all of us, and she was one who would always
be called a "ram in the bush" for whenever, or whatever the
situation called for. I and Bert first met as students at Alabama
State University, and then later at Sanctuary, historically

Canaan Hill Missionary Baptist Church. Alberta's gift was seen immediately in her fellowship at Sanctuary. She wrote the Script, and narrated our annual Maundy Thursday program for several years. May we all thank God for allowing her to be in our presence.

# "My Pastor"

Looking back from whence he came,
To a flock he did not know.
But now today blessed we're able to say,
How much we love him so.

A lovely family that keeps him warm,
To lift him up in times of storms.
To urge him on to battle,
With hugs and words from the Psalms.

When I think of all the things he has done,
One thing I know for sure.
He teaches us all about God's only son,
And how in Jesus we shall endure.

**Bernard Mckenzie**

**This poem is dedicated to my Pastor, Ossie T. Brown Jr, and all Pastors. Being a pastor of a Church is truly a charge, and a work of God. One must be empowered by the Holy Spirit because of the many struggles, personalities that come to diffuse the work of the kingdom of God. Pastors need encouragement from families, as well as church members. They need to be loved and appreciated.**

Let the elders that rule well be counted worthy of double honour, especially they who labour in the word and doctrine.
1 Timothy 5:17 [KJV]

# "Remember Them"

Surely as life moves on, we lose so many in the faith,
And yet we realize that to all of us, death won't wait.
I remember Mother Copeland and Mother Aver heart were
saints who set the pace,
They were always on a mission before they finished their race.

Velma Rogers gave us poems and was always ready for battle,
But sister Gwen Westry was one you really couldn't rattle.
Sister Vera Brown would always say "Just do what God said
to do,
And in time they will all be rejoicing around God's throne
anew.

These saints set standards of how we should love and trust
God,
Never backing down from their faith when things got hard.
They left us a legacy of how to never let our light go dim,
This Is truly the reason why we will always remember them.

**Bernard Mckenzie**

This poem is written as a tribute to 5 deceased members of
Sanctuary "Historically Canaan Hill Missionary Church" in
Montgomery, Alabama where Ossie T Brown Jr Is the Senior
pastor. They were truly strong women in the faith and their
work before God and the ministry will never be forgotten

Mrs. Jessie Copeland
Mrs. Azalea Aver heart
Mrs. Velma Rodgers
Mrs. Gwen Westry
Mrs. Vera Brown

# "Just Do What God Says"

Why do we read the Bible and say this book is good?
    Was it because of something you read, and you understood?
What does it mean to say this is God's way,
    If we don't believe it and don't obey?

Since creation, God's word has always been the same,
    God doesn't lie, nor does He change.
His words you hear or, the words you read,
    Promise blessings and directions to those who believe.

Why do we look for a harvest when there is no seed?
    Abraham was told to leave home as God had decreed.
His obedience and faith led to many blessings old and new,
    We like Abraham, and others can live a life of blessings if we "just do what God say to do."

**Bernard Mckenzie**

This poem is a tribute to Sis. Vera Brown deceased wife Of Dr. Paul C. Brown Sr. Sister Vera was truly an angel that God blessed us with during her time on this side of heaven. She was a devoted wife, mother, a servant of God and her legacy will live on in her children and many who served in ministry. She would always say no matter how much you read the Bible it does us no good if we don't obey it. She would say and I quote "Just do what God says" The Book "Just Do What God Says" in remembrance of her was written by her husband Dr. Paul. It can be purchased on several different sites. It is a tremendous book.

22 Do not merely listen to the word, and so deceive yourselves. Do what it says. James 1:22 [NIV]

# "The American Red Cross™"

Not enough praise is given to those we can count on indeed,
They volunteer their time, talents, and resources to help those in need. No storm, war, or catastrophe will alter their plans to be on time,
To see that red cross on that white flag is one-of-a-kind.

Life in general is full of trouble and will visit all in some way,
But each morsel of help rendered gives hope for a much better day.
It benefits us all to give blood and support their mission of grace,
They will be there for us no matter what obstacles we face.

They are always there in our gloomiest days and nights,
Always focused on their mission serving God's mercy and light. Certainly, they are God's earth angels, when properties, lives and all seem lost,
We are more than blessed to have as friends, The American Red Cross.

**Bernard Mckenzie**

This poem is a tribute to The American Red Cross. Their mission is to prevent and alleviate human suffering in the face of emergencies by mobilizing the power of volunteers and the generosity of donors. We are so blessed and fortunate for their service.

16 And do not forget to do good and to share with others, for with such sacrifices God is pleased. Hebrews 13: 16[NIV]

# "Care Givers"

Who are these people who care for those who need a hand?
They always go beyond the call of duty to help every man,
Whether it be a spouse, family, or friend in dire need,
Always giving care and love that God calls a good work indeed

Who are these earth angels that put themselves sometimes in harm's way?
They are sometimes exhausted and for them, we must pray
It's not easy to care for yourself and the needs of others we love,
For their strength and faith must come from God above

Who are these people who themselves are burdened with this labor?
Yet, they never waver or complain but always show godly Favor
Oh Lord please give them the strength to continue to serve those in need,
Their work will never be forgotten, and with you they will succeed

**Bernard Mckenzie**

This poem is a tribute to those who work and serve their loved ones in sickness and are sometimes the only caregiver who can cater to their needs. This also goes to those who work in hospitals, nursing, and assisted living homes for the elderly, and Hospice There is an underlying factor that sometimes the person giving the care is under stress unknowingly. Today, there are many workshops and different ministries that help caregivers through support and encouragement Dr. Paul C Brown Sr wrote a book called "Count It All Joy" Reflections

71

of A Caregiver In this book he wrote of his experiences and how he was able to depend on God for his strength Dr Brown was the caregiver to his deceased loving wife Vera He embraced the covenant of marriage and committed himself to the care of his wife until her passing "In sickness and in health" to him was not an optional phrase. He counts it all joy James 1 2-4

# "FOR WHOM THE BELL TOLLS"

*He was a humble servant who carried out his call.*
*Proclaiming worldwide why Jesus died for us all*
*Never giving in to his suffering in this life.*
*John Paul II preached that we cannot live in strife*

*He traveled the world to encourage the flock.*
*Preaching that it was God's love that sent Jesus our rock.*
*His message of reconciliation, mercy, and love,*
*The Pope knew it was the will of God our Father above*

*Though he requested his memoirs be buried in the earth,*
*His legacy will always be of great merit and worth.*
*Yes, Pope John Paul II certainly touched our souls,*
*For on the day of his Homegoing celebration, men will say,*
*This is the man, For whom The Bell Tolls."*

### *BERNARD MCKENZIE*

This poem is written in memory of the late Pope John Paul II, the Spiritual leader of the Roman Catholic Faith, a worldwide Christian Denomination. His mission and work was that of a servant's role. He preached that Jesus our Lord and Savior died for all men and that those who receive him as their Lord must be examples of that same love.

# "The Real Superman"

Forever we will remember how he bravely stood,
    So very tall and handsome when life was good.
But sickness came to take him away from all the glory,
    Now there will be no more movies, just a real-life story.

He never gave up fighting for a way to end the pain,
    But this fight continues, his death will not be in vain.
The cure he proudly fought for, will one day receive its dues
    And others will benefit, from what he bravely pursued.

Oh yes, I remember the movies, and Superman was the best,
    Even on the screen he fought for justice, but now he rests.
Physically we won't see him again, on this earthly side.
    But we will never forget the race he ran, the days before
he died.

No kryptonite or sickness will ever harm him again,
    He soars in his heavenly home where life will never end.
Thank you for all the memories of how you took a stand,
    To us Christopher Reeves, you will always be" The real
Superman."

**Bernard Mckenzie**

This poem is a tribute to a real-life superhero, Christopher
Reeves was a gifted actor who played the Marvel hero
Superman. He was a wonderful human being who died on
October 10, 2004, from complications from being paralyzed
from a horse-riding accident. The years before he died, he
became a voice and spokesman for research involving
paralysis.

# "Ossie"

Never was there anyone in recent times,
That poetically dramatizes the integrity of a race.
Though he now rests in the hands of the divine.
We will never forget the dream that he chased.

To see a people stand proud and erect.
For he knew we must move from the past
This was his legacy to defend and protect.
The proud history of a people now free at last.

A lovely family he leaves to cherish the memories,
And a wonderful wife he loved for many years.
Ruby, we love you, and like you, we all agree,
That your husband and our friend was so dear.

Who now will peak for us, for injustice and strife?
Who will tell them that we deserve the right to be?
Though you're gone from this side of life,
Ossie, we know you're in Heaven saying, Lord, please help
my people to be free.

**Bernard Mckenzie**

This poem is written in memory of the late Ossie Davis, a poet,
actor, civil rights activist, and producer. His voice was one of
power and grace. He spoke as one whose purpose was to
encourage and defend his people and to educate the world
about the integrity, history, and significant contributions of
black Americans.

# "The Voice"

I will never forget the years of my youth,
Especially listening to artists that spoke the truth.
Yes, the rhythm and singing sounded so good,
Even though some of it I never understood.

But I knew music was something I wanted to do,
So, there I was in the bands trying to imitate you.
Now I know the gift God gave you is for you alone,
And no one on this earth can imitate your songs.

As I became older, I began to listen more clearly,
I heard messages in your songs that moved me dearly.
Your stand on injustice and how love is a better choice,
Made me realize that your songs are more than music it's a voice.

**Bernard Mckenzie**

Written in tribute to Stevlan Hardaway Morris better known as Stevie Wonder, one of God's gifts to man. His music in my eyes transcends the essence of music and its ability to make a difference in the lives of a people, or a nation. The messages in his works touched the inward parts of our culture such as racial injustices and inequality. He looks to sing about the things that will bring peace, harmony, and love as he believes God wants us to. Though He may be physically blind he sees more than most of us will ever see.

# "A Man Called Ray"

Oh, thank you, God, for devices that replay the memories,
For when I hear Ray Charles, without them, it would be a
tragedy.
For many years he blessed us with his unique songs,
But now he sings where only the righteous belong.

Family, friends, and admirers alike,
Will miss Ray's big smile and his use of the mic
He never met a stranger and was always genuinely kind,
Ray Charles was truly a hero and an advocate for the blind.

The US Hymn America will never be sung right again,
Only Ray Charles could make you feel it within. Yes,
we will miss him, but his legacy lives today,
Because when I hear his music, I know it's Ray

**Bernard Mckenzie**

A tribute to the deceased artist Ray Charles. He was truly one
of the most profound and prolific music geniuses of our time.
He was versatile in many different styles, Jazz, Rhythm and
blues, Pop, Country, or whatever. The music didn't make Ray,
but Ray made the music.

# "Remember 9/11"

It was a day we'll all remember so well,
   The day when two of America's Icons fell.
Going about our daily routines and asking ourselves,
     What does this mean?

Parents seeing their children off to school before work,
   Not knowing if they will ever see them again on this earth.

I will never forget the sorrow and destruction we beheld with
   our eyes, Vowing vengeance is coming with a swift reply.
The first responders and all who rushed to give relief,
    Suddenly found themselves under a mass of rubble and
heap.

It was a day that the heart of America stood still,
   Many questioned God, Lord is this your will?
New York, New York, the world prays for you,
   Be not dismayed, we're here to help you get through,

A day when men began to search their souls,
   Looking unto Thy creator who shapes and molds.
We will never forget our loved ones, not one day in seven,
   In our minds and hearts, we will always "Remember 9/11

**Bernard Mckenzie**

In memory of the many lives that were lost on that tragic day
September 11, 2001

# "Early"

They run and jump like deer in the spring,
  Young eyes that are excited about everything.
They have no problems now because life is fun,
  Soon they will find out what trouble lies under the sun.

The friends and laughter and never having to pay,
  For health and welfare, they'll experience one day.
The time that passes is like a puff of smoke,
  For them, life is fun now but soon it will be no joke.

So run along children jump and play some more,
  For trouble will certainly visit you, it knocks on everyone's door.
It's best to know the Almighty God, and learn about the truth,
  Only He can order your steps, in the days after your youth.

**Bernard Mckenzie**

"Remember also your Creator in the days of your youth, before the evil days come and the years draw near of which you will say, "I have no pleasure in them", before the sun and the light and the moon and the stars are darkened and the clouds return after the rain." Ecclesiastes 12:1-2 [KJV]

# "It's Not Bad To Grow Old"

The days of my youth passed by so fast,
Everything was fun, and life was a blast.
Finally, I realized that time would not wait,
Things I should've done, and now it's too late.

Like a young eagle, so high did I soar,
Climbing each new height, more and more.
My mother once told me, enjoy my youth,
Now I can say, it was nothing but the truth.

So many years, God watched over me,
Through the toils of life, too foolish to see.
I'm very thankful that God's hand kept me whole,
Now I know, "It's not too bad to grow old."

**Bernard Mckenzie**

Even to your old age and gray hairs I am he, I am he who will
sustain you. I have made you and I will carry you, I will sustain
you and I will rescue you. Isaiah 46. 4 [MIV]

# "Love Just Hit Me"

Finding a compatible mate wasn't something taught,
At each shared meal you learn things that can't be bought.
A few times of laughter like a previous date before,
Hoping that this date will not be another closed door.

Now you ponder about what does this mean,
It starts like embers before a fire, yet low, but seen.
Rolled up in time the embers become like an inferno,
And now a burning desire to see them so much more.

A path that seems to be guided by a hand of miraculous power,
A heart that is filled with excitement, each day, and each hour.
You feel like a fighter who weaves and gets hit by a punch he
did not see
And after getting up he says to himself...I just realized that
love just hit me

**Bernard Mckenzie**

This poem reminds me of my early years of dating and the
process of getting to bond with someone compatible. Some
dates were just dates but when the right person came along it
was something different and before you know it you were
really in love.

# "Why"

I don't know why I write,
Is it like a climber who reaches for the highest height?
I guess I'm trying to know more about the inner me,
To say it's not enough to write about what I see.

The countless hours that I stay awake,
  Never knowing how long it will take.
Sometimes I never know what to write about,
  My fingers just start writing whatever comes out.

I Just don't know why I write so much,
  I hope one day I will get the touch.
Maybe, someone will read what I wrote and get something out
of it
  For now, I'll just keep writing until someone says, you need
to quit.

**Bernard Mckenzie**

# "The Dusty Bible"

I was dusting my shelf in the spring of May and came across a book that was as dusty as could be.
I sat down to see what it had to say, and now for the life of me, I can't stop reading what I see.
It talked about a God and all that He has done, through prophets of old and about His son,
I was sad to see those He loved didn't obey His laws and found themselves making bricks with straws.

But I was amazed that despite how the people disobeyed Him, He forgave them and delivered them as such.
I read many stories of His miraculous fame, and yet they all seemed to mention a savior who came.
One who would save a world so dead in sin, and then be restored to God again. You know I think I will dust this book off and keep this book somewhere next to my side. It seems like the more I read it, the more I seem to abide.

**Bernard Mckenzie**

16 All scripture is given by inspiration of God, and is profitable for doctrine, for reproof, for correction, for instruction in righteousness:

17 That the man of God may be perfect, thoroughly furnished unto all good works

2 Timothy 3:16-17 (KJV)

13 He has delivered us from the domain of darkness and transferred us to the kingdom of his beloved Son, 14 in whom we have redemption, the forgiveness of sins. Colossians 1: 13-14 [ESV]

# "First Responders"

Through the rain, fire, storms, and all travail that toss and take life,
Are precious souls who come to our rescue like paper cut by a sharp knife.
Do we ever think that they have regard for the loved ones they leave behind?
Not ever thinking that this is the last call they will ever make or find.

When the two New York towers fell on September 9/11 it was something to behold,
We all watched in disbelief thinking it was a movie trailer waiting to be sold.
Men, Women, Children and all who lost their lives on that dreadful day in September,
Can never be brought back to us but their story we will always remember.

Those who dashed out in their rescue vehicles and attire to save those in need,
Found themselves victims of the same fate and mortars of evil deeds. Their stories will always help us to appreciate those who answer the call,
God bless our first responders, we honor them in life, and even when they fall.

**Bernard Mckenzie**

This poem is a tribute to the many first responders who put their own lives on the line to save and rescue so many from the many circumstances that take lives. Our Fire and Rescue, Police and Emergency Medical services do so much to save lives and we are and should be grateful for their service This is something that we all can appreciate and thank them for the work and service they give

# Chapter Six

## "A STILL QUIET VOICE"

Most of us have read the poem "Footprints." From its reading, we know that God is always with and near us. In times of grief or guilt for a sin committed, we feel as though we are all alone. Remember Elijah in Kings 1: 18 and 19, after the great victory on Mt. Carmel between Jezebel and her wicked prophets of Baal, Jezebel sent a messenger to Elijah and told him that he would be killed. Elijah being distraught and afraid ran for his life. There in the wilderness, he asked the Lord to take his life for he was no better than his ancestors. So, the question is? How can one of God's mightiest prophets who had just been used to claim a great victory, succumb to threats from pagan worshipers? In essence, it can be said that most of us will experience similar circumstances after great triumphs in our lives. In Elijah's lament, God's glory [shecinah] descended upon the mountain and God spoke among earthquakes and storms. He spoke in a still quiet voice, thus, giving Elijah the reassurance and courage to continue his mission. Even in our greatest fears, God is with us, and we must continue to do the work He has commissioned us to do. When Jesus gave His disciples the Great Commission in Matthew 28 19 - 20 He told them that He would always be with them even until the end of time. The book of Peter 1. 5, reminds us to always be aware of our adversary's [Satan] tactics to make us feel like God has deserted us. The second part of Hebrews 13.5 states: "He Himself has said, I will never leave you nor forsake you" (NKJV) Listen to his voice, it's as soothing as a mother's voice to an infant child. God's word is life and He will speak to you in your moments of doubt and discouragement.

## "You Are Always Thought Of"

Never think that you are all alone,
    Life's journey is full of dangers unknown.
Surely all of us will experience days of pain,
    But rest assured that Jesus Knows your name.

Your family and friends are concerned about how you are feeling,
    They give words of encouragement and pray for your healing.

God says He has loved us with an everlasting love,
    For this reason, you are never forsaken but always thought of.

**Bernard Mckenzie**

**3** The LORD appeared to us in the past, saying I have loved you with an everlasting love, I have drawn you with unfailing kindness Jeremiah 31:3 [NIV]

# "Broken But Still Blessed"

How arrogant are we?
With our heads in the sky,
Never repenting for our evil deeds.
As time passes by.
But surely as we live,
Each day at our best.
There will be a day,
When we shall confess.
I'll never forget the days of my trials,
Saying Lord why me? as I went through self-denial.
Now humble am I, with my head lowly at rest,
For a moment I was "Broken but Still Blessed."

**Bernard Mckenzie**

**9** If we confess our sins, he is faithful and just and will forgive us our sins and purify us from all unrighteousness. 1 John 1:9 [NIV]

# "It's Still A Good Day"

The shadows of a dawning day,
Breaks free of the night before.
Only to bring the newness of life,
A radiant light that all life adores.

Yesterday's memories never seem to fade away,
So let the healing start here and now.
Because no matter what happens, it's still a good day.

The seasons change without our permission,
They need no reminder to change.
So why do we keep holding on to the past?
When nothing remains the same.

Every day presents another chance,
And though some things in life don't go your way,
Just thank God in spite of it all, it's still a good day.

**Bernard Mckenzie**

This is the day which the Lord has made; Let us rejoice and be glad in it. Psalm 118:24 [KIV]

# "Gone But Never Forgotten"

Indeed, no words could ever heal your hurt.
The memories and laughter you shared on this earth.

God knows the pain that you feel.
And yet we still ask, Lord is this your will?

We shall all wither as leaves in the fall of the year,
Only so much time to spend with those who are so dear.

We take for granted, that our days will never end,
Make sure you say "I love you, again and again.

Take joy in knowing that they are in a better place,
Waiting to see us when we finish our race.

For now, remember those precious moments,
When you feel down and lonesome.

Even though they're gone,
But in our hearts, they will never be forgotten.

**BERNARD MCKENZIE**

So also, you have sorrow now, but I will see you again, and
your hearts will rejoice, and no one will take your joy from
you **John 16:22** [NIV]

"He will wipe every tear from their eyes. There will be no
more death or mourning or crying or pain, for the old order of
things has passed away **Revelation 21:4 [KJV**

91

# "You Are Never Alone"

As we live each day in life's sudden toils,
      We come to know that today's freshness is tomorrow's spoils
The flight of honeybees is truly a wonderful sight,
      As they carry strands of pollen that enhance new life.

As our loved ones rest in their heavenly home,
      The fond memories of them come sometimes when we are alone.
Never forget the creator of all things knows your pain,
      When the earth is dry it is He that sends forth rain.

No words can completely ease the sorrow you feel,
      But this is a time of hurt and a time to heal.
As you journey through unknown circumstances,
      Always remember in our savior Jesus Christ you are never alone.

**Bernard Mckenzie**

16 And I will ask the Father, and he will give you another advocate to help you and be with you forever-17 the Spirit of truth. The world cannot accept him, because it neither sees him nor knows him. But you know hir for he lives with you and will be[a] in you. John 14: 16-17 [NIV]

# "It's Not The End"

One day we will come to the end of the road,
No more shall we have to carry life's heavy load.
Sickness and trials that may have caused our demise,
There will be nothing to abort the plan in our creator's eyes.

How we live on this side will determine our way,
To heaven or hell, when Jesus returns that day.
Your faith in him will guarantee your tomorrow,
Deny him and become a recipient of eternal sorrow.

This life of trials will define who you are,
Each person must choose to follow their guiding star.
Let Christ be yours, your star, and your friend,
And then you will know "It's Not the End."

**Bernard Mckenzie**

Jesus told him, I am the way, the truth, and the life. No one
can come to the Father except through me John 14:6[NLT]

# "Being Holy"

Why do we revisit those things that constantly defile us?
To constantly be fooled by this flesh we trust.
Knowing that our flesh is weak and easy to give in
Often disobeying the Holy Spirit within.

Tell me how many times we have forsaken our words
Living a life in God's eyes that's absurd.
All men are tempted to do what we know is wrong.
But yet we wallow in Godly sorrow singing a sad song.

Our obedience demands all of our true grit,
For our adversary, the Devil knows what we struggle with.
We must continue to pray for strength so we can live right,
For only in Christ can we possess the power and might

**Bernard Mckenzie**

But just as he who called you is holy, so be holy in all you
do, for it is written. "Be holy, because I am holy." 1 Peter 1:
15-16 [NIV

# "Jesus Saves"

There are times when you're going through a storm,
    And there's nothing in sight to embrace.

Isn't it plain from the pain that's written all over your face?
    But then suddenly the storm becomes calm and there's lightning shining upon the waves,

As you drift ashore your pain is no more,
    Because once again you realize that Jesus saves.

**Rufus Mckenzie Jr.**

Taken from My deceased brother's book" Poems of Faith" Copyright 1991

Jesus stood up and commanded the wind, be quiet and He said to the waves, be still the wind died down, and there was a great calm. Mark 4.39

# "My Personal Friend"

I communicate with my personal friend when I'm feeling
tired, lonely and even when I'm in despair,
And I know, when there is no one else to talk to He will
always be there.

My faith is very strong and if I do what is right,
Then nothing can go wrong.
I communicate with my personal friend at least two or three
times a day,
Simply because I want to become close to Him, in every
possible way.

Some call Him God, some call Him Jesus,
Some say He's the creator of all mankind.
But deep within my heart, I can call Him a personal friend of
mine.

**Rufus Mckenzie Jr.**

Taken from My deceased brother's book..." Poems of Faith"
Copyright 1991

"I call you friends because I have told you everything I heard
from my Father. John 15: 15, [GN]

# "The Peace Of God"

The riches of the world cannot heal the problems of life,
Those who have abundant treasures know the word strife.
The jewels, machines, and all we humanly bare,
Are material in nature and can't possibly care

Solace may be found in a peaceful walk in a park,
Or the staring of the stars in the moonlit dark
Fame or fortune is no guarantee that life won't be hard,
But only true inner comfort is the peace of God.

**Bernard Mckenzie**

6. Be anxious for nothing, but in everything, by prayer and petition, with thanksgiving, present your requests to God. 7 And the peace of God, which surpasses all understanding will guard your hearts and you minds in Christ Jesus. Philippians 4. 6-7 [BSB]

# "Just Believe"

Though some days may seem dark and dreary,
God's powerful hands keeps you from becoming weary
Nothing that hurts you can stand against His might,
For His mercy delivers in the darkness of night.

He who watches over Israel never slumbers nor sleep,
He watches over you while you mourn or sleep.
The victories I've had are not my story,
For my God, my Father deserves all the glory.

Sometimes your family and friends and all who care,
May never know the problems you bare.
But your Father in heaven hands are open to receive
He only tells us that all things are possible, just believe.

**Bernard Mckenzie**

Jesus said unto him, If thou canst believe, all things are
possible to him that believeth. Mark 9: 23 [KJ]

# "Lord Make Me A Puppet"

Lord, If I were a puppet, I would have no choice but to obey, feeling every pull from your string and obeying every word you say.

Lord, If I were a puppet, how could I not rejoice, seeing thy awesome power and to hear thy loving voice?

Lord, If I were a puppet, I would be guided by your hand without shiver or sway,
Lord, make me a puppet to obey every word you say,
Lord, make me a puppet so I would have no choice but to obey.

**Bernard Mckenzie**

"But this is what I commanded them, saying, 'Obey My voice, and I will be your God, and you shall be My people. And walk in all the ways that I have commanded you, that it may be well with you." Jeremiah 7.23 (NKJV)

# Chapter Seven

"Documents of Injustice"

These poems are poetic expressions concerning my view of America and some of the racial injustices that are so prevalent in our country. I still believe that we are a nation blessed by God, but we must recognize that the color of a man's skin should not make him a bullseye for injustice. I also addressed several issues concerning the impact of, particularly Hurricane Katrina. Mankind throughout the ages has always faced catastrophes of enormous devastation. In the early centuries, it was the Black Plague, diseases, droughts, and storms of great destruction. Recently it's been earthquakes, 9/11, the Tsunami, and now Hurricane Katrina. Some disasters are acts of Governments, such as Nazi Germany and the terrorist acts of Al Qaeda, and other sadistic groups. Hurricane Katrina highlighted some serious issues that I saw as injustice. Our unpreparedness and act of apathy to our fellow Americans mostly African Americans was an act of treason and betrayal. To call our own people refugees is absurd.

This storm also moved the hearts of people who went above and beyond governmental issues, or racial boundaries to aid afflicted and suffering people. It serves notice that even countries whom we as a government might disagree with came to help in this effort. Why do we need a tragedy to foster this goodwill? The recent problems of gun violence, the mass shootings, and so many innocent victims shot by the police and so many other atrocities are no longer hidden. Other American immigrants whether they are Jewish, Iranian, or other

100

nationalities have also been scrutinized and discriminated against.

In conclusion, I think all of us can learn something about what's more important; idolizing earthly possessions and pride or, living a life where men can work out their differences along political and racial issues in harmony. There have been so many wars and so many lives lost. Things can be replaced, but the lives that are lost is a great tragedy. God has a way of opening our prideful eyes to what He sees as unacceptable behavior. Surely, we can all learn something, and with God's guidance and strength, we can all love and try to live the right way. God put us here to love, and to treat our fellow man with honor and dignity regardless of color. Until we understand and adhere to his purpose for us and choose His ways, we shall never have peace only turmoil. Homes and possessions can be rebuilt and regained, but the question is. What about the hearts of people?

# "Exposed."

America, America, God's grace does shine on thee,
Land of the pilgrim's pride, the land where our fathers died.
Though we say this in our song is God's grace truly shining
on a nation that has no
empathy nor sympathy for its people?

The excellence of righteousness that portrays her glory,
Became an open book for the world to see the real story.
A man's skin color or lack of wealth is still an indictment
against him. and though there is hope, the outlook still looks
grim.

Suffering Americans called refugees in their homeland,
Many who saw it wondered, is this America or Afghanistan?
Will equality in America ever reign, only God knows.
But one thing I do believe is that the real America is what
Hurricane Katrina exposed.

**Bernard Mckenzie**

# "Lessons Learned"

What lessons did we learn about Hurricane Katrina a storms
of the ages?
Did we summarize it by saying that the people needed to live
above sea level or poverty level?
The poor, whether white or black and all who stayed or were
unable to leave,
Became the victims of a bureaucratic mess of land besieged.

What lessons did we learn about people and their regard for
one another?
Did we not recognize that those who suffered the most were
people of color?
The justice and help they thought would someday arrive,
Was just a dream washed out as a wave in the Gulf Coast
tide.

What lessons did we learn about this type of catastrophe and
human suffering?
Didn't we not see that when people become desperate, they'll
do thing to survive?
The things we take for granted like brotherly love and
compassion for others,
are more precious than silver and gold... So, what did we
learn?

**Bernard Mckenzie**

# "The Lady of a Storm"

The Weather experts monitored Katrina's path and growth
from the African coast,

Not yet knowing that she would be the storm, to bring
suffering the most.
With a name that sounds delightful and full of grace,
would soon disrupt the lives of millions regardless of race.

She raked the Caribbean, only showing part of her wrath,
then like a child skipping across south Florida who stood in
her path. South Florida thought that she was supposed to be
just! a Category 1, But they will tell you that she was really a
"son of a gun."

She leaves there and grows up to be a lady in the Gulf of
Mexico, Kissing the oil platforms for Shell, Amoco, and
Texaco.
Now she unleashes her fury on the coast of three other states,
as if it was a bad relationship, saying, these places I really do
hate.

The Weather experts said Katrina was just about as perfect as
a storm could be,
Her eye was so round and pretty, and she was big, and far as
the eyes could see.
Yes, a Category 4 she came in, and though we were
forewarned,
No Hurricane in recent memory has ever destroyed so much,
as "this lady of a storm."
But they will tell you that she truly was a son of a gun.

**Rev. Bernard Mckenzie**

# "Refugees"

Never in history has a storm displaced so many, with such devastation,
but in August of 2015, Hurricane Katrina humbled this great nation. Nothing could stand in the path of her power,
and because of Katrina, families were scattered, heavily laden,

The scenes we witnessed brought scars and disbelief to our eyes,
to see children, the poor and they somewhat despised.
To them, it seemed like eternity before anybody came to their rescue, ironically, this tragedy will forever warm governments what they must do.

Yes, assistance finally came pouring in from all over the world, and the nations pondered,
How could America let this happen to its people, and we all wondered?
It's understandable for displaced Americans to be called evacuees,
but how in the world could we call our own people Refugees?

**Bernard Mckenzie**

This poem was written in response to the devastating hurricane that happened in Louisiana and other surrounding states is August 2005. Many of the victims lot everything and many today have relocated all over the nation never to return to the state or home they once knew.

# "Pictures"

A picture of pets displaced by Hurricane Katrina was a sight
to see, Being that they were seated, and transported to see, on
air condition buses was no, problem to me.
But when I saw people transported standing up on open
trucks in scorching heat like hogs,
It was then I realized that something was wrong with this
picture of the dogs.

Tell me how humans whom God created, and gave
dominion over all living things on earth,
Be treated less than animals whom they raised from
birth.

Do these pictures imply that there is a presence of racial
injustice to be fought? or what I saw was people who couldn't
afford to ride the bus...............I don't know, tell me. This
was the picture I saw.

**Bernard Mckenzie**

# "America"

Where is this land of the free, and the home of the brave?
A land where immigrants came over the waves.
From the ends of the earth seeking a new opportunity
And yet they ask, where is this sweet land of liberty?

Those who lived here before the ships set sail,
Lived in peace, and harmony, gathered honey, and ate quail,
They had no worries wants or fears,
And yet they would soon be led down a trail of tears.

Many were brought here unwillingly to work fields of cotton,
Treated worse than animals and always forgotten.
Beaten, stricken with no hope of glory.
Freedom is a never-ending cry and still a present story.

Yes, some climb walls hearing of this land,
A new frontier and destiny for every man.
This country like no other claimed love and freedom
Although it's grand, it is no Garden of Eden.

People from all over the world formed this nation,
And in its infancy, there were many trials and tribulations.
Maybe one day we can live up to who we say we are,
That all men are created equal, but are we?

**Bernard Mckenzie**

# "Now We Know."

Now we know that our country is not what we dreamed,
A place of liberty, equality, and justice that rolls down like a
stream. The injustices and things that were hidden in the past,
They have strangled us like vapor from volcanic gas.

Now we know that a man's skin color means to win or lose,
To be driven, beaten, and even killed with no way to choose.
Families separated because of not bearing a national flag,
Brought here as slaves and treated as a filthy rag.

Now we know that this flag is just a piece of cloth,
Showing stars and stripes covering up the many lives that
were lost. The pictures we see now are images of what has
always been.
The so-called land of the pilgrim's pride stricken with racial
sin.

Now we know we can't hide from who we say we are,
The shade has been lifted and the light has revealed the dark.
Though our blood is red like all people God created,
Yet we know that we are still mistreated and hated.

**Bernard McKenzie**

# "Enough is enough"

A people so despised and treated without dignity or class,
Because of their color were going nowhere fast.
Scrutinized, chastised, and horror without end,
Simply because God put a little color in their skin.

December 1, 1955, a late fall day in Montgomery Alabama,
A quiet and humble black woman define the word courage
and stamina. Tired and weary, she gets on city bus to go
home,
She refuses to give up her seat and then came the storm.

She was arrested and taken to jail for not giving up that seat,
Her defiance gave birth to a movement and led to Jim crow's
defeat. This was at a time when life for blacks was extremely
tough,
But because of Rosa Park and others we will remember when
they said "Enough is enough."

**Bernard Mckenzie**

This poem is a tribute to Rosa Parks and other blacks who
were instrumental in igniting the civil rights movement doing
those turbulent years. Montgomery Alabama is largely
considered the birthplace of the movement. The bus boycott
set the stage for a young minister at the time who became the
leader and like a Moses for civil rights. This was the late Dr.
Martin Luther King Jr.

# "Martin's Dream"

I remember that day watching that black and white T.V. so well, Suddenly, a Special News Bulletin flashed about a great man who fell. Slain because of his stand for equal rights; not only for blacks but for all men,
Never will I forget that moment ever again.

The injustices he fought for have caused men much pain,
For all men, regardless of color are in God's eyes the same.
The vision he spoke of in Washington D.C., was a glimpse of what God says will one day be.

Though we still live in a world where people are hateful and mean,
We must continue the fight and remember the dream.

**Bernard Mckenzie**

*In tribute to Dr. Martin L. King, a man inspired by God to fight a peaceful war against racial discrimination, an injustice that plagues our society. His fight for civil rights is today still an ongoing battle. Though he was slain for his fight, the dream still lives on, and we must still root out those things that oppress people.*

# "Immigrants"

Oh, America why are so many immigrants crossing our
border?
Who told them that this was a place of law and order.
Was it you that got them here because of the chief labor,
And now, hello they have flourished and become your
neighbor.

Who can blame any people for not wanting more out of life,
Especially when the land they left is full of strife.
And yes, we say to them go back home where you belong,
And then we realize we need someone to work cheap, to
work long.

They come from every nation to this land of milk and honey,
Looking for new opportunities to live and to make money.
Yes everybody is upset which seems so insignificant,
Maybe we need to ask the Native American Indians about
who all are called Immigrants.

This poem highlights the struggles we have as a nation
considering any who crossed our borders and not be a citizen
of the state. There is no reason why we should close our eyes
during this national concern, but we must be fair and
courteous in our laws and ways to handle this crisis. We must
not forget that all of us at some point in time besides the
native Americans came from another country.

**Bernard Mckenzie**

# "Something Is Wrong"

A Child lying in feces, hungry and dying.
That is why I believe that somebody is lying.
How can a world laden with great resources and riches,
Allow children to starve while landing on planet Mars and its
ditches.

The elderly work until death to survive,
Wasn't it they who made it possible for us to thrive?
Is it right to turn our back on them and walk away?
Or shall we provide welfare for them in their remaining
days?

Why hate a man because of color and culture,
Then waiting for his death like a desert vulture.
To see our youth living their fantasies in a demonic song,
This is just one of many reasons I believe "something is
wrong."

**Bernard Mckenzie**

# "Colorblind"

I have no problem with being called names,
  For God created us and respects all men the same.
Even though my color may dictate some things,
  I will not fear, for the Lord God is my king.

People need not look upon the color of a man's skin,
  So how is it that you call them an enemy and not a friend?
Believe it or not, all men are truly related,
  From the first family, our beginning was stained with
hatred.

Jealousy, envy, death, and all that we have sown,
  Will have no place in heaven so let this be known.
Whatever problems you may have in accepting each other,
  Love is the only way, and in God's eyes, there is no color.

**Bernard Mckenzie**

Then Peter opened his mouth, and said, Of a truth I perceive
that God is no respecter of persons: But in every nation he
that feareth him, and worketh righteousness, is accepted with
him. Acts 10: 34-35 [KJV]

# "Why am I Black?"

*Are you less than a man because of the color of your skin?*
*To be ridiculed, scorned, and problems without end.*
*To be the last hired and the first fired,*
*And then working three jobs and saying I'm tired.*

*Black man the ways of the world shouldn't be new to you,*
*Was it not your parents who taught you to make do?*
*This struggle is real, and we must pray to survive,*
*Surely, God wants all of His children to thrive.*

*Do you know why trees are green and roses turn red?*
*And who makes sure that all living things are fed?*
*Who helps the birds migrate their way back?*
*It's simply the same God who knows why I am black.*

**Bernard Mckenzie**

# "I Wish I Was White"

If I were white, I know everything would be alright,
No needs and worries, and no need to fight.
The first in line wherever I go,
and the last to be oppressed, stricken and poor.

If I was white, the flag would be my victory,
but being black, I see only a dark history.
If there was a choice of color to be born right,
I would have chosen to be white.

If I were white, life's choices would be so many,
but being black I see very little if any.
Though it was just a thought to be white and great,
I have no choice but to be black and filled with hate.

I wished I was white and free to be first
No long lines of waiting, and separate fountains of thirst
and though it was just a thought, or perhaps a dream in the night
But so much misery and hate, makes me wish I was white.

**Bernard Mckenzie**

# "The Gun"

Bullets riddling through the air care not where they go,
Aimed or fired with the intent to harm, it does not know.
Yes, we know there are many valid reasons to own a firearm,
Protection of home, nation, and other reasons that will cause
harm.

Since its creation, its power caused devastation,
And its deadly beauty is common to all people and nations.
For protection, hunting, or even as a collector's jewel,
Even to men of high status who thought it was right to duel.

Children cheerfully play cowboys, cops, and robbers,
Sadly, many become victims that lead to family sorrows.
The gang bangers and all who think it's a big deal to carry
one,
Only produce coffins that may one day carry them.

Now we must carry, bury, and pray for the day it will end,
For surely, its intended purpose was not to make friends.
It was created to kill, maim, or whatever happens under the
sun,
In most cases, it's never a good ending when you hear about a
gun.

**Bernard Mckenzie**

# "War"

For what reason or purpose, do we fight or behave?
Is it persecution, land, or something we crave?
Are we saying that life is nothing to live for?
Shall we continue to hate without love anymore?

Families and nations that are horrifically blown apart,
By the greed and pride of those who care not.
Over many years we have certainly seen much blood spilled.
Never can it be compared to love, peace, and goodwill.

Death, destruction, and all that we see,
Reminds us of how far we are from harmony.
Sadly, since the beginning of time, we've seen many battles,
No nation has escaped this awful thing we call "War."

**Bernard Mckenzie**

**Why do wars happen?**
There is rarely one single, clear cause of conflict and,
ultimately, war. The causes of a war are usually numerous
and can often be intertwined in a complicated way.

Many theories have been put forth over the years as to why
wars happen, and some of the greatest minds have offered
their take on the subject. What is your take?

# "Shoot First and Ask Questions Later"

All too often we've seen people killed because of racial
profiling
And some jumped to conclusions and said a gun was
showing.
Why is it that so many officers that are sworn to protect us?
Act like executioners that we are too scared to trust.

I dare not say that all our trusted servants seek to bring death,
Some are trustworthy and will help even if it's their last
breath.
But even amid those who serve us well,
Lurks the evil that is only found in the pits of hell.

Yes, the next time I'm confronted by the law I will not move,
I will gladly show my hands for I have nothing to prove,
For I know in time we all will stand before our creator,
I just don't want to be a victim of "shoot first and ask
questions later."

**Bernard Mckenzie**

This poem is a tribute to those who have lost their lives
because of a misunderstanding with some of our citizens who
are sworn to uphold the law. I do believe perhaps some of
these incidents are warranted because of a quick response
and sometimes mistakes do happen. But many of the
incidents we've witnessed are acts of racial injustice and
cannot be tolerated. Many years ago, these kinds of acts were
not seen because of technology but, today everything is seen
and documented. I also want to commend and support our
officers who uphold the law and do it with honor and
integrity. Surely, we need your service, but we must weed out
those who use the shield to create mayhem.

# "Mass Shooting"

Why are we shooting each other as if it was the right thing to do?
These shooters have no regard for human life even theirs too.
It looks like the age limit is of no concern for their evil intent,
Men, women, and children all fall victim to a mind that is bent.

O Lord, help us to live a life of peace and regard for each other,
Where we can learn to love and not kill or shoot one another.
So many dreams and lives have been lost because of deranged minds,
For these killers have given up and happiness, they won't find.

Lord, I pray that those who have been taken away from us too soon, Have a place of rest in you and never again see gloom.
Let's pray and always be watchful for the evil that lurks among men, Maybe we can help save them, and tell them that taking a life is a sin.

**Bernard Mckenzie**

This poem is a tribute to the victims who lost their lives because of shooters who targeted and randomly went on a shooting spree in different locations in our nation and even abroad. Our Schools, Malls, Stores, and even places of worship were victimized by shooters who for whatever reason, whether it was a mental issue or racial shot and killed innocent people. May God have mercy on them and let us continue to support and pray for the families who lost loved ones.

# Chapter Eight

"Paradise Regained

Finally, as with any musical composition, or scale there is beginning and end. In a musical scale there are seven different notes and the last is like the first. As it was when the first man and woman Adam and Eve lived in Paradise to live forever to enjoy the blessings God had prepared for them. But because of Satan's trickery and their disobedience led to the downfall of man and we have had trouble since the beginning because of our sin nature. But our loving God our Father from the beginning of time made a way that we would get back to Paradise through the shed blood of His only begotten Son, Jesus Christ. John 3:16

Because of Christ we have been restored and redeemed once again to have eternal life and live in paradise with our loving God, Father and creator of heaven and earth. Like a musical scale each note has a purpose as each circumstance in life we encounter can alter our destiny and outcome. These poems depict many areas of our lives that question our faith, to see if you have decided to receive Jesus Christ as your Lord and Savior and inherit the blessing and promises that God has for us. This book may not be a read for those who care nothing about religion or have no desire to look at their spirituality in terms of the destiny of man. But one thing is sure that man being a living soul will exist even after the physical has passed away. There will be only two choices for eternal life heaven or hell. My prayer is that, if you are standing at the crossroads of life and have not made a decision, prayerfully these poems may offer some inspiration and encourage you to move out in faith. Ephesians 2: 8-9... For it is by grace you have been saved, through faith-and this is not from yourselves, it is the gift of God-not by works, so that no one can boast. Additionally, Romans 10:9-10 states that, if you confess the Lord Jesus Christ with your mouth, and believe in your heart that God raised Him from the dead, thou shall be saved. Acts 4: 12... Salvation is found in no one else, for there is no other name under heaven given to mankind by which we must be saved. May God bless you as you read these poems in "Poetic Reflections in the Key of Life

# "A Friend Indeed"

No one stands alone in this world we live,
God created us with hands that receive and give.
A song, a hug, or words that encourage life,
To a broken heart that has been pierced with a knife.

A true friend accepts you as you,
No explanations are needed to do what they do.
Their work is of love, and not glory or fame,
This love is from God whose love is without change.

Since we've all sinned and fallen short of His glory,
No one can boast because we all have that story.
Troubles, problems, or whatever it might be,
A friend like Jesus, is a friend indeed.

**Bernard Mckenzie**

1" stanza of the hymn "What a friend we have in Jesus"

1.  What a friend we have in Jesus,
all our sins and griefs 10 bear
What a privilege to carry
everything to God in prayer
O what peace we often forfeit,
O what needless pain we bear,
all because we do not carry
everything to God in prayer

# "I Will Give You Rest"

The burdens we bear can weigh on our minds.
It comes to all men, and some by design.
This load that you carry, could be one that you built,
Don't throw your head down, and wallow in guilt.

Jesus is our salvation, and yes, He does care,
No problem is too hard, that He cannot bear.
He's calling on you, I pray you will confess,
Come to me, all you who labor and are heavy laden.
And "I will give you rest."

**Bernard McKenzie**

Come to Me, all you who labor and are heavy laden, and I
will give you rest. Matthew 11: 28[ NKJV]

123

# "The Greatest Gift"

He created all things at the speaking of His voice,
The songs of birds and even the trees rejoice.
The sky, the sea, and all creatures near and below.
Even the creepy things that we despise so.

The heavens, stars, and what lies far above our heads,
Even the buzzards are cared for and fed.
The cry of newborn life rings throughout the earth,
For all living things will replenish through birth.

Events and circumstances rest in His hand,
Nothing is more precious to Him than the creation of Man.
When I think about all the miraculous things God has done,
His greatest gift to us was Jesus His Son.

**Bernard Mckenzie**

Thanks be to God for His indescribable gift. 2 Corinthians
9:15 (NIV)

# "What Matters The Most"

Is life worth living just to waste away?
    When each second shortens our days.
The things we say we will do tomorrow,
    Might happen if it was time we could borrow.

Our purpose in life is not in things material,
    Man's eternal destiny is only achieved in what is spiritual.
God's grace is freely given which gives us no reason to boast,
    And a relationship with Jesus is truly the only thing that
matters most.

**Bernard Mckenzie**

*For by grace are ye saved through faith, and that not of
yourselves: it is the gift of God

Not of works, lest any man should boast. Ephesians 2: 8-
9(KIV]

# "Faith In Jesus"

When death comes, how will you be?
  Will your faith be grounded in thee?
There will be many tears on this earthly side,
  But everlasting Joy awaits those who abide.

We run this race as best we know,
  Knowing the evil one runs to and fro.
For a man, woman, boy and girl,
  There will be no pity in this sinful world.

Yes, live your life but put your faith in Him,
  For there will be a time when our lights go dim.
Only God knows the day of our sorrow,
  But your faith in Jesus will guarantee a heavenly tomorrow.

**Bernard Mckenzie**

Do not marvel at this, for an hour is corning when all who are
in the tombs will hear his voice and come out, those who
have done good to the resurrection of life, and those who
have done evil to the resurrection of judgment. John 5:28- 29
[ESV]

# "Jesus Is Coming Back"

The veil has been lifted for all eternity,
Man's way back to God happened there at Calvary.

The words of our Lord, as God called Him home,
He said in a little while your comforter will come.

He goes to prepare our home and our crown,
We must tell everybody about the love we've found.

Just stay in this race firmly on the track,
We know not the day nor the hour, but Jesus is coming back.

**Bernard Mckenzie**

And behold, I come quickly, and my reward is with me, to give every man according as his work shall be. Revelation 22:12 [NIV]

My Father's house has many rooms; if that were not so, would I have told you that I am going there to prepare a place for you. John 14:2 NIV]

# "Confess"

So many wonders God has made,
    A world of miracles, the sun, and the shade.
He created for his divine pleasure,
    But man is His fondest treasure.

He gave him dominion over all his creation,
    To care for the earth through love and dedication.
Somewhere in paradise, we defied the hands that made us,
    To be kicked out and forever struggle to regain His trust.

But because God so loved us, He sacrificed His only
begotten son, Jesus was crucified and rose again, now
salvation is available to everyone.
Shall we not believe, and our lips not confess,
    Damnation is sure, and hell will be our new address.

**Bernard Mckenzie**

that if you confess with your mouth the Lord Jesus and
believe in your heart that God has raised Him from the dead,
you will be saved. Romans 10: 9 (NKJV]

# "In Jesus Name, I Pray"

I call for thee oh precious Lord.
I call upon thy name.
With a bowed head and humble heart,
In you, there is no shame.

The toils of life will come our way,
No one can escape its wrath.
But every day in you I pray,
My Lord who lights my path.

The storms may rage, and the winds shall blow,
But my Savior will guide my way.
In Him, I've found a resting place,
And "In His Name I pray."

**Bernard Mckenzie**

Whatever you ask in my name, this I will do, that the Father may be glorified in the Son. If you ask me anything in my name, I will do it. John 14: 13-14 [ESV]

# "Tell This Story"

The Angelic Choir song before his birth,
That man may have peace in God's seed,
Three days He laid down in that tomb,
Thirty-three years after coming from Mary's womb.

He was born to die on the cross,
For such sinners were we,
God never charged for what it cost,
For His grace was given free.

Yes, He was lifted for all to see,
That we may see His glory,
That God's son came down for me,
That I may tell this story.

**Bernard Mckenzie**

13. And suddenly there appeared with the angel a great multitude of the heavenly host, praising God and saying: 14"Glory to God in the highest, and on earth peace to men on whom His favor rests!" 15. When the angels had left them and gone into heaven, the shepherds said to one another, "Let us go to Bethlehem and see this thing that has happened, which the Lord has made known to us."... Luke 2: 13-15 [NIV]

# "Jesus Did That For Me"

I'm certainly not worth the price He paid,

Even though I'm so wonderfully made.

Jesus gave his life up on Calvary.

Sometimes I wonder why He did that for me.

His love for us is holy and without blame,

Looking beyond our sins and treats all the same.

I stood there and watched him on that tree,

Asking myself why he did that for me.

He was abused and treated like scum,

Beaten until his pain became numb,

This kind of love is only from God almighty,

Because God loves me, Jesus did that for me.

**Bernard Mckenzie**

But God demonstrates his own love for us in this: While we were still sinners, Christ. died for us. Romans 5: 8 [NIV]

# "Jesus Is Worthy"

Are we worthy of God's mercy because of our disgrace?
Stained with the stench of sin before a Holy God we couldn't face.
But God's plan of redemption demonstrated His great love toward us,
Sending His son to die for what he created out of the dust.

Who could have given this type of love that was never earned,
laying down His life for a world that is destined to burn.
No, we are not worthy of any praise, mercy, or glory,
But what Jesus did at Calvary makes Him more than worthy.

**Bernard Mckenzie**

Saying with a loud voice, "Worthy is the Lamb who was slain, to receive power and wealth and wisdom and might and honor and glory and blessing!" Revelation 5:12 [ESV]

# "The Christmas Tree"

When I look at a Christmas tree.
   I think of how it came to be.
For me, it's a reminder of what we know,
   About Jesus who came to save us from hell below.

The ornaments and lights remind me of how we were lost.
   It was at Calvary that Jesus' blood decorated that cross.
But oh, thank God that we celebrate this day of the year,
   Jesus Is God's greatest gift to those far and near.

As we sing cheerful songs about who's naughty or nice,
   Remember it is Christ's birth and his sacrifice.
As we love, serve, and tell others about God's love for thee,
   Let us always remember this when we see "The
Christmas Tree."

**Bernard Mckenzie**

For unto you is born this day in the city of David a Saviour,
which is Christ the Lord. Luke 2:11[KJV]

# "Never Thirst Again"

The dear pants along a life-refreshing stream,
Finds relief and serenity in waters that redeem.
They will come there until their life will end,
But in Jesus, you'll find that this is where new life begins.

The things we cherish only last so long.
This present life and laughter will all be gone.
Drink of His water no matter how thirsty you have been,
Eternal life is yours, and you will "Never Thirst Again."

**Bernard Mckenzie**

But those who drink the water I give will never be thirsty
again. It becomes a fresh, bubbling spring within them,
giving them eternal life." John 4: 14 [NLT]

# "No More Bye Bye's"

It is without saying, that the loss of a loved one is hard to
bear,
    The days and nights without them to share.
Even the thought of this may be more than you can stand,
    But know that every man must tread this barren sand.

May you find comfort in knowing that your joy is not forever
    gone, For this life is only a transition to a much better
    home.
The God who created us knows the days of our labor,
    And those who have received His Son Jesus have found
favor.

So, for now, just walk with the memories of years gone past,
    Knowing that these mortal bodies will one day breathe it's
    last.
For within us lives a soul that will never die,
    And one day never again will you have to say "Bye Bye."

**Bernard Mckenzie**

"For while we are in this tent, we groan and are burdened,
because we do not wish to be unclothed but to be clothed
instead with our heavenly dwelling, so that what is mortal
may be swallowed up by life. Now the one who has
fashioned us for this very purpose is God, who has given us
the Spirit as a deposit, guaranteeing what is to come. 2
Corinthians 5:4-5 [NIV]

# "Only Jesus"

Those who look for the keys to success,
Will only find temporary solutions at best.
Even when we take a chance to wait until tomorrow,
Sometimes our guarantees are intercepted by sorrow.

Nothing is more precious than God's love for us,
Only He can promise that in Him our treasure won't rust.
Before His coming our situation was very dim,
Now all of our sins are forgiven through Him.

God showed mercy and compassion because God is love,
For this reason, He sent His only Son from above.
No other name is given to men to save us,
We were so messed up that it took the Lord Jesus.

**Bernard Mckenzie**

There is salvation in no one else! God has given no other
name under heaven by which we must be saved." Acts 4: 12
[NLT]

# "Victory In Jesus"

At the moment when man first opened his eyes,
God held him like a mother with a newborn child.
Adam and Eve were told like God they would be wise,
By the Devil who is the father of all lies.

But a merciful and loving God set our redemption in motion,
And even in our disobedience, he took care of our needs.
His Son came with power, love, and spiritual devotion,
And now salvation is found only in Jesus to those who
believe.

Jesus set the example of how we should live,
His entire life the Son of God was without sin.
Although they crucified him on the cross, he asked God to
forgive. Now through him, life is everlasting, and the sting of
death would end.

**Bernard McKenzie**

But thanks be to God, which giveth us the victory through
our Lord Jesus Christ. 1 Corinthians 15:57 [KJV]

# "Light A Candle For Me"

I asked that you light a candle for me,
  One that will never burn out.
Because without you dear Lord,
  There have been many moments of doubt.

I'll pray dear Lord that the candle becomes an everlasting
fire,
  If you plant the seed, I'll fulfill the need of your desire.

If you light the candle,
  I will feel like the humblest servant ready to serve.
A privilege I'll feel I've deserved.

In my heart, I know that you've set me free,
  Thanks, dear Lord for lighting a candle for me.

**Rufus Mckenzie Jr.**

Taken from My deceased brother's book..." Poems of Faith"
Copyright 1991

"You are like light for the whole world. Your light must shine
before people so that they will see the good things you do
and praise your Father in heaven: Matthes 5: 14a &16b [GN]

# "He Is The One"

We make too many distinctions concerning our call,
  We say we are Methodist, Catholic, Baptist, and all.
We act as if religion is rooted in our denomination,
  Realizing that some of this is man's creation.

Jesus Christ died for all men on earth,
  And only in Him shall we receive new birth.
Heaven's eternal life comes only through Christ,
  Salvation is by faith in Jesus and no other man or device.

In spite of all the arguments to say what is best,
  Let's look at the truth and put our differences to rest.
As we see the day approaching, for the return of God's only son
  All men will then know that He is the one.

**Bernard Mckenzie**

19 that at the name of Jesus every knee should bow, of those in heaven, and of those on earth, and of those under the earth," and that every tongue should confess that Jesus Christ is Lord, to the glory of God the Father. Philippians 2: 10-11 [NKJV]]

# "The Master's Plan"

All too often a man thinks he has the answer to the world's problems, Only to realize without God, we cannot solve them.
Though Philosophy and Science may have its place,
Nothing is ever fixed right without the sovereignty of God's grace.

God's word is his plan for how we can thrive and live,
For all things are purposed by him and his grace he willingly gives. To learn the meaning of God's eternal plan is found in the Bible,
It is his will, his word, and his plan for our survival.

Jesus, God's Son was in the beginning and called the word,
God's plan of salvation is granted to those who believe what they hear.
That Jesus was born, bled, and died to be raised again on the third day,
Only in Jesus Shall we inherit eternal life, a new heaven and earth, and a better way.

**Bernard McKenzie**

Remember the former things, those of long ago; I am God, and there is no other, I am God, and there is none like me. I make known the end from the beginning, from ancient times, what is still to come. I say, 'My purpose will stand, and I will do all that I please. Isaiah 46: 9-11 [NIV]

# "So, I, Can Come On Home"

Help me dear Lord, hear my plea,
   Help me keep my feet on the ground.

Where I am blind, help me see,
   So, I can once again become heaven bound.

I pray dear Lord, that you reserve me a seat,
   Somewhere round your throne.

Let me know when my journey is complete,
   So, I, can come on home.

**Rufus Mckenzie Jr.**

Taken from My deceased brother's book..."Poems of Faith"
Copyright 1991

"There are many rooms in my Father's house and I am going
to prepare a place for you. John 14:2[GN]

# "Now Is The Day"

Lord Jesus were we worth the stripes you took on the cross?
  Maybe it would have been better for us to be forever lost.
The suffering, pain, and all you did for man,
  And yet we haven't tried to understand.

Lord Jesus, surely you are the reason why we sing,
  No other hand is worthy that we may hold and cling.
God's love for us was your great sacrifice,
  Yet it's sad that a man's heart can be cold as ice.

Lord Jesus, your mercy is available and without end,
  I am so happy and thankful that now I'm called your friend.
I will tell my story to all in my path and my way,
  I know many will say to wait until tomorrow, but I will tell
them that now is the day.

**Bernard Mckenzie**

For He says: "In an acceptable time I have heard you, And in
the day of salvation I have helped you." Behold, now is the
accepted time; behold, now is the day of salvation. 2
Corinthians 6:2 [NKJV]

# "The Way It Was Supposed To Be"

Originally God created man to live forever,
In paradise in peace, love, and harmony together.
For Adam and Eve to fill the earth as God decreed,
That was the way it was supposed to be.

But the choices they made, and now we die,
For God told us the truth, the serpent told a lie.
Like sheep, we all had gone astray,
But thanks be to the Lord our shepherd who showed us the
way.

Yes, His staff was broken, for you and me,
What a price Jesus paid at that place called Calvary.
Now we can peacefully return home and live eternally,
Truly, that was the way it was supposed to be.

**Bernard Mckenzie**

All we like sheep have gone astray, we have turned everyone
to his own way, and the LORD hath laid on him the iniquity
of us all. Isaiah 53:6[KJV]

## "The Splendor of Heaven"

Nothing on this earth can compare to what awaits you in
glory,
And though we've read about heaven it's only part of the
story.
Gold chains, rings, and diamonds we wear so proudly and
bold,
It will be like the dust swept off streets paved in pure gold.

The celestial capital will need no sun or moonlight for us to
see,
The light will come from the presence of God who will
always be. We can't imagine our home being prepared by the
lamb who was slain,
Waiting for our arrival and a new mansion that adorns our
name.

A river of life flows from God's throne to the new heaven in
its creation,
Along the banks shall be planted a tree of life that's healing
for the nations.
In heaven, we shall not worship just one day but in our time
all seven,
Yes, these things and this earthly life can't compare to the
"Splendor of Heaven."

**Bernard Mckenzie**

- In my Father's house are many mansions: if it were not so, I
would have told you. I go to prepare a place for you. John
14:2

And he shewed me a pure river of water of life, clear as crystal, proceeding out of the throne of God and of the Lamb. In the midst of the street of it, and on either side of the river, was there the tree of life, which bare twelve manner of fruits, and yielded her fruit every month: and the leaves of the tree were for the healing of the nations. **Rev. 22: 1-2 [NIV]**

# "The Only Way"

To reclaim the glory, we enjoyed in paradise,
was a plan God installed without our advice.
He commanded them not to eat from the forbidden tree,
For He said death will surely come and paradise you must
flee.

Now blood must be spilled to atone for our sins,
Jesus God's son paid the price, our savior who calls us
friends.
and yes, we thank God for His mercy after we failed to obey,
for us to regain paradise, believing in Jesus is "The Only
Way.

**Bernard Mckenzie**

For God so loved the world that He gave His only begotten
Son, that whoever believes in Him should not perish but have
everlasting life. John 3:16 [KJV)

That if thou shalt confess with thy mouth the Lord Jesus, and
shalt believe in thine heart that God hath raised him from the
dead, thou shalt be saved. Romans 10:9[KIV]

Neither is there salvation in any other: for there is none other
name under heaven given among men, whereby we must be
saved. Acts 4: 12 (KJV)

# Little About the Author

Born and raised in Miami, Florida, on June 14, 1954, to Rufus and Alberta Benecken McKenzie. His Father, Rufus McKenzie was also a prominent blues artist as well. Some of his father's recordings have been cataloged and can be purchased on Apple Tune. Bernard displayed a gift of music that was first known while attending Allapattah Jr. High School under the direction of the late Mr. Herbert Rhodes, who was the Band Director at that time. He started playing the Euphonium, a lower brass instrument. Through practice and his love for music, Bernard became one of the most coveted musicians in his age group, winning multiple awards locally and statewide. He then attended Miami Jackson High School under the direction of the late Mr. Jacob Muscanera and the late Mr. Erick Knight, who was also a prominent local jazz pianist as well. Bernard continued to excel in High School and won multiple awards in performance. It was Mr. Eric Knight who inspired Bernard to learn to play the trombone because he would have more opportunities to perform with different groups than playing the Euphonium. Upon suggestion, He worked hard and became proficient and played trombone his last year in High School. He went on to college at Alabama State University in Montgomery, Alabama, in 1972, where he majored in Music and performance. He played in the marching band, symphonic band, Jazz, and brass ensemble groups throughout college. While in College, he also performed with a local group called the Oasis II Band from Selma, Alabama, a very prominent rhythm and blues group that could play Jazz, rock, and just about anything. Bernard learned jazz improvisation and became very proficient and sought after. While in college he also achieved many awards. Who, who in American Colleges and Universities, The John Phillip Sousa award for most outstanding musician and many others.

Bernard, aspiring to write songs, discovered he had a gift for writing poems and continued to write and became more interested in his newfound gift. Bernard also became more interested in religion, and a friend named Vanessa Goodwin and her family led him to Christ in Selma, Alabama the year 1976. He gave his life to Christ and was saved. Several years later, in Montgomery, after serving in a local Church, he became a Deacon. This was when he began to write poems based on life experiences and events that happened in his and our lives and what it means to love and trust God. As if it was enough, Bernard was called to be a minister of the Gospel in 2001; since then, he has been an associate pastor at the Sanctuary Cannan Hill Missionary Baptist Church under Senior Pastor Ossie T. Brown Junior. At present, Bernard has received his Master's and Doctor degrees in Biblical Exposition from Andersonville Theological Seminary.

Bernard is presently a Member of the Montgomery Symphony Orchestra and has been for over 30 years. He is happily married and now resides in Montgomery, Alabama, as an artist in residence and a minister of the gospel of Jesus Christ. It was his love for music and the grace and love of God that inspired him to write this book of poems.

# Acknowledgments

I must begin by thanking my God for using me as a vessel to compose this work. It would be impossible to even think or attempt to do such a work without his guidance and inspiration. Special love goes out to my lovely and caring wife, Addie, and my little Booby my son Elijah. I must recognize my multi-talented son Jason and my lovely daughter Princess who were so instrumental in my early recognition of the importance of the family. I thank God for all my family. My lovely sisters, Mommie, Jackie my nephews, nieces, my lovely Grandchildren and so many wonderful in-laws. Special love also goes out to my mother, Mrs. Albertha Benekin Mckenzie the joy of my heart. In my upbringing, she was always an example of faith during hard and lean times. Special recognition to my deceased father, Mr. Rufus Mckenzie who was inspirational during my early years in becoming a musician. I'm sure my musical talent was inherited from him. Thanks to my Pastor, Ossie T. Brown Jr. for his spiritual guidance, and my wonderful church family, at Sanctuary/Historically Canaan Hill Missionary Baptist Church for all their love, encouragement, and prayers.

I thank God for the inspiration from my deceased brother Mr. Rufus Mckenzie Jr., who was also a poet and has a published work of his own called "Poems of Faith". As a tribute to him, they are included in this book Thanks, Junior for setting the mark. Thanks, Stevie Wonder for giving me the concept which was taken from his Album, "Songs In The Key Of Life". This concept allowed me to orchestrate these poems into a harmonic framework depicting various life experiences.

I would like to express my sincere gratitude to Alabama State University in Montgomery, Alabama for providing me with musical education that allowed me to integrate rhythm and depth into this literary project.. Many, many thanks go to Mrs. Hilda Swain who inspired me to do something with these poems almost twenty years ago. The compilation, editing, and grammatical work involved in this work could not have been realized without her expertise. Thanks, Hilda, I know you are God sent. To all of you, family, friends everywhere. Love and may God continue to be the key to a blessed life through Christ..

www.ingramcontent.com/pod-product-compliance
Lightning Source LLC
Chambersburg PA
CBHW060858280326
41934CB00007B/1102